ACT THE PART!
GET THE PART!

Make yourself a power professional

LINDA REED FRIEDMAN

Published by Advanta Book Group Press

Allentown, PA 18104

All rights reserved.

No part of this book may be reproduced, stored in a retrieval system, or transmitted by any means, electronic, mechanical, photocopying, recording, or otherwise, without written permission from the copyright holder.

Distributed by Advanta Book Group Press
For ordering information or special discounts for bulk purchases, please contact
Advanta Book Group Press, POB 1343, Allentown, PA 18105
814-360-1950

Design and composition by Advanta Book Group Press
Editor Michael Sheehan, Marketing Messages
Cover Design by Joellen Reichenbach, SelectSalesPA

Friedman, Linda Reed
　　Act the Part! Get the Part! – Make yourself a power professional / Linda Reed Friedman. – 1st ed.

ISBN: 978-0-9862301-0-2-51850

1. Business Presentations. 2. Leadership 3. Creativity 4. Negotiation   5. Image   6. Time Management   7. Etiquette   8. Speaking   9. Planning   I Title

Printed in the United States

First Edition

ii

TO:

My Mom – Ruth
who said
"You got that determination from me"
She was right!

and

My Aunt - Hannah Harrison
who with her scottish accent
would say.
"You can do anything you want girrrrll."
She was right, too!

Contents

Preface   v
Acknowledgements   xii

I. Being a Power Professional   1

    Chapter 1.1 Image Bearing   2
        Image - Inside, Outside and Perceived
    Chapter 1.2 Conventions   33
        Customs and Etiquette

2. Being a Power Professional Manager   47

    Chapter 2.1 Leading your Team   48
    Chapter 2.2 Simple Leadership Tips   67
    Chapter 2.3 The Control is in Time Management   81
    Chapter 2.4 Negotiation   93
        Preparing for a successful negotiation

3. Being a Power Professional Leader   112

    Chapter 3.1. The Power is in the Plan   114
    Chapter 3.2 Creativity   123
        The Foundation of Your Growth
    Chapter 3.3 - Verbal Communication   133

Conclusion   145
References   151

Preface

Why did I write "this" book? I wrote it for you because you need this information -- and because I couldn't find it.

I kept looking for this book. You know, it's the book that had the "how to" answers. The little black book I knew for sure that the rising stars in corporations had hidden in the bottom drawer of their desk. The little black book that it seems they were born with. How did they get that book and I didn't? Who gave it to them? Who wrote that book? Where could I find it? I looked in the library, book stores, and even a used book store in an antiques mall. Surely, I thought, someone had put a few guidelines together!

Sadly, the little black book of guidelines didn't exist. The "How To" book about being a powerful, successful person was nowhere to be found. I've met brilliant people, talented and educated people, but they didn't have the book. They were working on becoming powerful and successful, but they were also looking for the book.

Why do you need the information in this book? Because to be successful, you need to know how to think and how to behave in a variety of circumstances.

Preface

Our parents/care-givers did the very best they could to teach us those lessons. You're reading this book because you know there is more you can do and more you need to know to do it..

"Go for it," "Be the best you can be.". My Nana would say, "You can do whatever you set your mind to doing." I believed her and so should you. She was right!

On my journey, I found the little black book.

It wasn't really a book, though. Some of it was written on scraps of paper that were handed to me under the table at meetings. Some of it wasn't written – it was passed on to me by a female friend who tapped my leg to let me know I was blabbering. I found the ideas in this book tucked under seats along with the chewing gum at networking dinners.

And I found it at the receiving end of the virtual two-by-four that was hitting me over the head, saying "First we'll get your attention." The school of hard knocks also gave me a lot information but there was no textbook for the course.

The book also grew out of my life experience as a child, an adult, a wife, a mother, and a successful

Preface

business woman and entrepreneur who was making her way through the corporate world.

I've had a successful life. It's been more powerful than I could have ever imagined at times and often more fun than a party of 15-year-old girls laying on the floor with their heads on each other's stomach. There were times in the learning process that were more tender and sweet than the softest candy cotton but there were other times tougher and harder than a bed of nails.

My journey started with a promise that was stamped in my mind -- Dad said we were going to go to college. We were going to be the first. He died when I was eight, so he didn't get to see the results. When I graduated high school Mom said: "Apply for a job at AT&T -- everyone gets a good job there." After a one-day experience of typing for a temp agency, I went home screaming. Mom asked, "What? You want to go to college?" And so I went off to college. It took me 6 years, full-time and part-time. I was first in the family to earn a college degree and I went on to enjoy my first job as a grade school art teacher.

With a BA degree in art education and an associate's degree in Interior Design, I stumbled out of college and into a job. I never applied anywhere. I got phone calls, I was needed. I said to myself, this is going to be a good life.

I married and we moved across country to California and I found another teaching job. We were living the high life. We flew back and forth from New Jersey to California.

Our life then took a few nasty turns here and there but we survived them all. We're still married after 45 years— a reminder that love is a daily decision and that some days it's easier than others.

To shorten this tale, the journey took me from making money any way I could, to having it roll in faster than I could count. To earn money early in our marriage, we sold art work paper Mache pigs and photographs at arts and crafts shows. We sat under an umbrella to protect us from the sun and rain. Then I became a district manager selling decorative copper at home parties and then I created a company to sell window treatments. That helped to pay for our new kitchen.

I learned about interior design by working for free at a kitchen cabinet supplier. I turned that experience into a part-time job at a high-end interior design firm. I worked in their back room office, which was in the

Preface

basement. I sat next to the water heater and in front of the washing machine and typed on a portable typewriter.

Then after a dreadful short stint at a furniture dealership, I was able to move into corporate management, as manager of space planning and interior design.

Building on all this experience, both positive and negative, I created The LRF Design Group, Inc. a commercial interior design firm.

My volunteer work for both the business and service communities helped to build my knowledge base. I learned how to run my business better, how to build a team and how to lead a group. But, to become a leader, I needed a vision of what I wanted to contribute and how I wanted to grow an organization.

So, as I was growing my business, I also served in leadership roles in a wide variety of organizations, including the American Society of Interior Designers, the International Facility Management Association, the Hunterdon County Chamber of Commerce; the Chamber of Business & Industry of Centre County, and the Greater Lehigh Valley Chamber of Commerce.

I also served in Rotary Club as a faculty member of the Leadership Institute, as President of my Rotary

Preface

Club and as Rotary Trainer for District 7350, earning the "Service Above Self" Award. I became a member of Toastmasters International and served as Vice President of Education, as President of my club, as Assistant Governor of district 13. Along the way, I became an award-winning speaker.

I also created Investing in Ourselves, an investment club now almost 20 years old. And I became a health-care clown.

The Learning Guide

What I learned through all those experiences is that it isn't that hard if you have the book. If you are willing to do a few exercises to practice for an event or experience, you can be in control of your career.

This book is about giving you a practical guide you can use as you navigate today's workplace.

You will be reading and learning about -
Planning, Goals, Objectives,
Strategies, Creativity, Leadership,
Time Management, Team Building,
Trust, Confidence, Ideas.

Preface

In addition, you'll learn how to be a tender cheerleader, how to keep your cool and make it fun, when and how to be outrageous, how to prepare to negotiate, when and how to act tough in a business meeting, how to brand your image using fashion tools, and how to be your authentic self. And, possibly most important, how to be comfortable speaking in public.

To help you, there is also a workbook filled with exercises.

Summary:

You may know some parts of this book like the back of your hand or you may not need to read it at all. Other parts may be so unfamiliar to you that you will want to use the workbook. It has exercises that will help you to navigate a variety of issues.

Acknowledgements

To those who said, when I closed The LRF Design Group, Inc., "go out and speak" and to those who also said ; "You need a book", especially Dr. Rev. Mr. William Sadler", Thank you. Thank you for the confidence you have in me and the support you've given me.

It has been a journey of many years with so wonderful people along the way. Among them I want to acknowledge a few special influencers in my life. They are in no special order. Kevin Bertone, for his sense of humor and rock solid values. He is a perfect example of you can do it! Art Barkman for the epitome of customer service, Bob Smith who taught me the rules of leadership in IFMA, Clare Rohloff, a behind the scenes motivator and creative spirit, Ron Subber who believed in me more than I did, Pat McKiernan for her steady balanced view, Richard Biever for removing the FUD (fear uncertainty and doubt) in performance and for the energy, courage and support - thanks lovey, to my Rotary Family who have given me opportunities and experiences beyond my wildest dreams. Carol Walsh, PDG who teaches us about transparency and who is the best person to have in your life, Joe White, PDG, Rotary

Acknowledgements

DG who shunned the rules and asked me to be his Trainer. To the IIO – Investing In Ourselves Investment group I started. It is still going after almost 20 years.

To the wonderful people in my Toastmasters family, Tammy Miller for the introduction to Toastmasters, Charlie J. Wilson Ph.D. for our collaboration of International Idea Harvesters, Cathy Jennings, No Pressure Networking for being a friend and reminding me we're in this together, Nancy Alauzen, for her great spirit and introduction to the National Speakers Association.

To the readers, all of you, a special thanks to Jack Hill who said "here's how you write a book" and to Sybil Stershic and Celeste Bebe, who read the ramblings.

To my editors and proof readers, Grace Reed, sister extraordinary! Without her help and dedicated efforts this would still be in the computer!

Michael Sheehan, the writing master, he has had my writing back for years. Mike was my voice, in Interior Environments newsletter published quarterly for The LRF Design Group, Inc. for almost 20 years. I am grateful for his friendship, support and good counsel.

I am influenced and grown by the writings of Og Mandino - His writings trained my mind to think

Acknowledgements

differently and therefore behave differently. The writings of Brian Tracy, Anthony Robbins, and many more have been on my listening /reading table for years.

I am inspired by people willing to take risks, my favorite quote below says it all.

> "Life is either a daring adventure or nothing at all"
> …Helen Keller.

I have been blessed with unconditional love from my parents and family. It is a priceless gift, it gave me confidence and courage.

Last but not least, there are two + people in my life who make it worthwhile. Jerry, the perfect husband. He was exactly what I wanted in a husband, smart, good looking, with a fabulous sense of humor and boundless support. Rebecca, our daughter who is brilliant, creative and a very funny lady; who recently married Oshin, an equally brilliant, creative and a very funny guy.

It is for all of you who have made this journey, fun, memorable, filled with humor and a special love. Thank you.

Being a Power Professional

1.1 Image Bearing

Image Bearing
Image - Inside, Outside and Perceived

1.1 Image Bearing

"You now have to decide what 'image' you want for your brand. Image means personality. Products, like people, have personalities, and they can make or break them in the market place"

…………David Ogilvy

1.1 Image Bearing

Bearing

"All that we are is the result of what we have thought. The mind is everything. What we think we become."
~ Buddha quotes (Hindu Prince Gautama Siddhartha, the founder of Buddhism, 563-483 B.C.)

Why would you want to create a bearing that gives you a powerful professional presence? I'm defining bearing as your posture, your stance, your gait and your behavior.

Because your bearing becomes your personal brand. Your personal bearing precedes you into a room, like the whisper of perfume. Your bearing and essence are like a second skin; you wear it all the time. Because of the way you present yourself, everyone knows who you are and what you want to accomplish. Your bearing communicates that.

The benefit of a good bearing is that it gives you the confidence you need to do the work you love to do,

1.1 Image Bearing

to become the person you want to become, and to succeed at every level you can imagine.

Good posture is a key part of your bearing. When your body is balanced internally, it creates a personal mindset. By managing your posture, you have the feeling of being in control -- and that is powerful!

Your bearing can also affect your accomplishments. Success comes to those who communicate success.

Bearing also shows your character. A good bearing can convey your moral, ethical strength. You may not be where you want to be yet, but a good bearing can let you "fake it 'til you make it," because it can change your thinking. And at some point in the future, you will no longer be faking it. The person you want to become has become you.

Bearing can also create your own breathing space. When you develop a good bearing, you also develop a protective shield between you and other people, a space that allows you to think before you speak or act. And that space can be like an invisible magic shield

1.1 Image Bearing

Your bearing can help you achieve a powerful professional presence. You can own your space or own a whole room by being fully present.

Being fully present means that you walk into the room and acknowledge the first person you see, perhaps with a handshake and a warm smile. Call them by name, if you know it. If you don't, introduce yourself. Then go around the room and introduce yourself to the others who are there.

Being fully present doesn't mean you are talking all the time. It doesn't mean interrupting a meeting or using it as a stage. It doesn't need to be loud and flashy. It's really just a quiet acknowledgment of each of the people present in YOUR room. Do that and you *own* the room.

1.1 Image Bearing

There are three images you need to think about -- your inside image, your outside image, and the image of you created by the people you meet.

Your inside (self) image consists of your personal integrity and character.

Your outside image consists of your exterior style and what you wear to support your image both at work and during your leisure time.

Your perceived image consists of how your look and behavior appear to others. They create this image from what you think, do, and wear.

The best examples of building inside and outside images are in politics.

A politician's outside image is based on what is called a presidential image. Politicians hire people to make them look good. They are coached on what to wear and when to wear it. From golf shirts to tuxedos, every option is evaluated. Which color makes them look healthy and vibrant even when they are exhausted? All kinds of issues regarding their outside image are analyzed, from length of their finger nails to the color of their hair.

1.1 Image Bearing

Their inside image, on the other hand, is developed long before they become public figures. Their character was formed by their family, faith, the people they met, and the ideas they embraced. To be successful in politics, their inside image needs to be strong.

Their perceived image, how they are seen by others, is often created by advisors based on market research. It includes not just clothes and haircuts, but also bearing, manners, gestures, eye contact, personal style, openness -- anything that would enable them to make a positive connection with the public.

In a sales workshop, I once did an exercise using each of the four personality types as described by Carl Jung: Sensing, Intuitive, Thinking, and Feeling. The participants made four columns under these personality types and were given a list of famous people. They were asked to categorize them under these four designations. They participants decided that a particular politician who was listed had qualities in all four personality types.

1.1 Image Bearing

That politician has been trained and coached to behave so he exhibits all the personality types. Each of the participants in the exercise thought he was like them, and had the same feelings, values and thoughts. Voting for him and supporting him was a natural conclusion.

Be in control of your Image

Cultivating your image is a key stepping stone to changing your career and your life. Defining your image puts you in control. Once you decide to accept responsibility for your image and your brand, you become a powerful professional presence.

It is your job to polish your image. First you need to figure out who your audience is. Are you going to a job interview or to a board meeting? Your outside image should be appropriate for the people you are going to see and the purpose of the meeting.

1.1 Image Bearing

For both men and women, the word "fashion" seems to lead to a feeling of dread. But "dressing for success" is one of the keys to achievement.

What does dressing for success mean? It means matching your appearance to the culture and the attitudes of the industry or the company that you are striving to join. For example: A fitness trainer would dress in a casual way that would emphasis his healthy lifestyle. In contrast, a banker would dress more conservatively. Dressing for success means dressing for the job you are looking to do.

In Alyce Parson's book, <u>The Power of the Seven Universal Styles for Women and Men</u>, she suggests adopting one or more of the seven styles that fit your personality, your needs, and your goals.

The seven styles are Sporty, Traditional, Elegant, Dramatic, Romantic, Creative, and Alluring. If you want to tailor your image, I urge you get this book. There are simple tests in the book; they are fun and easy to take.

. . Hugh Mose is the Manager of the Business Centre Area Transportation Authority in State College, PA. He has branded himself a professional. He always

1.1 Image Bearing

wears a suit, because It creates the visual authority he needs to have as part of his job.

At the same time, he shows his sense of humor by wearing outrageous ties. He wears appropriate designs for holidays, events, and just plain fun.

His has created a visual image that says, "I am a professional but I am also approachable. I know how to follow the rules but I also know how to have fun. You can talk to me."

It works. According to Daniel Hamermesh, Professor of Economics at the University of Texas at Austin, and author of Beauty Pays: Why Attractive People Are More Successful, men and women who are well groomed and have a pleasant appearance will earn $230,000 more over their lifetime.

Depending on what your job is, a suit and tie or a dress/skirt and jacket may not be necessary, but a look that matches your profession is. According to The Glass Hammer, a website designed for women executives, (http://www.theglasshammer.com) "There is strong statistical evidence to show that women who wear make-

1.1 Image Bearing

up in business get better jobs and are promoted more quickly."

A recent survey supports this. It showed that 64 percent of directors said that women who wore make-up looked more professional and 18 percent of directors said that women who do not wear make-up looked like "they can't be bothered" to make an effort.

Take note: It is not about looking pretty. It *is* about looking like you care enough to make an effort.

Dr. Daniel Crane is a chiropractor who knows firsthand about the importance of branding his business and his business attire. He once thought he could wear whatever he wanted in his office and that his patients would welcome his casual cargo shorts and Hawaiian shirt. They did not. He returned to khaki pants, white button down shirt and lab coat. He found that his patients wanted him to look like the doctor he is.

In the end, it's all about the image you wish to project.

1.1 Image Bearing

Why Have an Outside Image?

Costume historians suggest that we started to evolve a concept of fashion in clothing in the mid-14th Century. For over 700 years we have been working on our public appearance and continue to do so.

Cultivating a distinctive outside image is important so that people can identify you immediately. A recognizable outside image consists of your clothes, your grooming, and your attitude. This is your brand.

Can you describe your image? It may depend on where you work. In a conservative corporate environment, there is an accepted mode of dress that is different from a small, informal company. There is a style that is perfect for a corporate look. If you want to be a manager, you learn to dress like a manager. You will look professional and polished. You will fit in.

Wearing colors that are right for you is a huge start on the path to creating your exterior image. The right combination of colors can make you look healthy and vibrant. This applies to both men and women. Here's a source: <u>Color Me Beautiful,</u> by Carole Jackson,

1.1 Image Bearing

is a book that groups various color palettes based on an individual's coloring.

Use this quick test to help you decide which colors are best for you. Stand in front of a mirror and close your eyes. Put the material you are planning to wear under your chin. Open your eyes. If the first thing you see is your face, it's a good color for you to wear. If you see the material, it's not.

There are many reasons to adopt this method for choosing your colors. For me, I wanted to have a complementary wardrobe with mix and match compatibility. So that no matter what I choose to wear, I maintain the image I wish to project.

Here's an example of the impact of image. After returning from an Image Intensive course at the Fashion Institute of Technology and thinking I thought I knew it all after just a one-week course. I met a friend for coffee,

My friend pointed out a very powerful person from the business department of a well-known university, sitting a few tables away. She was wearing a black pants suit, which included a black blouse. She had a pulled back hair style, wore little makeup and no jewelry.

1.1 Image Bearing

The coffee shop was crowded but this woman went unnoticed. Her lack of any personal image made her invisible.

She was dressed in the traditional style of a lawyer or a banker. She did look professional, but she was not memorable. There was nothing about the outfit that represented *her*. Her personality was hidden behind the black suit. What message was she trying to send? She is sending a message of "I can't be touched, I'm invisible" and the underlying message "don't talk to me".

Now, take a woman wearing the same suit but one who has an energetic hairstyle, appropriate makeup, a scarf with lots of color, a brightly colored blouse and/or a large pin or bracelet. All these things display her personality. What message is she sending? She is sending, an "I'm ready to talk business" message.

You need to decide who you want to be in your business community. You have two choices. You can show off your personality through your clothing and subtle changes in your behavior within the accepted standards of your work. Or you can decide what you love

1.1 Image Bearing

to wear and find a job that supports that choice of clothing. :

A woman applying for an accounting position was having difficulty landing a job that matched her training and experience. She was wearing a stylish but quite snug sweater with so much bling it almost glowed in the dark. Although she was a very competent woman, her chosen occupation didn't fit well with what she liked to wear. If she wanted a job in a bank or an accounting firm, she needed to change her wardrobe to get the job or even a second interview. Banks and sweaters with lots of bling don't go together well.

. You have done the research, chosen a specific look for yourself, identified appropriate fabrics, colors and accessories that define you. When you use all these tools you add an energy to your look. Your look becomes your personality type, the one you have chosen. It is you!

I have a friend who frequently wears a yellow-green color that most people would shy away from, but ber red hair and blue eyes are the perfect match for those colors. To complement her business image, she

1.1 Image Bearing

---

strengthens both her image and her business by giving away pens and building a Web site that match her color scheme.

Accentuate + Camouflage = Balance

Nobody is perfect. To achieve the image you want for yourself, you need to accentuate your positive qualities and camouflage your negative qualities to arrive at a balanced look. Every part of your body can be accentuated or camouflaged.

Everyone has some feature that they want to change. I have a round face. To camouflage it, I apply additional eye makeup and darken my eyebrows. I changed my hair style to create a thinner profile and added dangling earrings. It was a small change, but I got a big result. The result was twofold. I saw my face as being balanced, orderly, therefore visually calmer. With a slimmer face, the cherub like visual reference was gone, I looked more mature.

If you are top-heavy, you need a visual foundation to make you look more stable. Accentuate your lower

1.1 Image Bearing

body with color – dark colors on the bottom, light colors on the top. Add a fuller skirt or fuller slacks.

If you are bottom heavy, you head often looks smaller. Unfortunately that can give people the impression of a smaller mind, no matter how smart you are. Solution: Accentuate the top. Dramatic makeup and a stunning haircut will keep the eye on the top. Add jewelry around your neck, wear a larger blouse or jacket or patterns.

Remember, you can camouflage the parts of your body you don't like by downplaying them visually.

My mother-in-law is a good example of how image can impact your level of success. Florence was an executive for the Estee Lauder cosmetic company. She was a brilliant woman but also traditional and thrifty. She had lived through the depression and raised two kids on pennies that had been stretched out so far they looked like copper thread.

As the Lauder Company grew, so did her responsibilities. She grew with the company and eventually had an office that was a windowed treasure in the General Motors Building overlooking Central Park in

1.1 Image Bearing

New York. She was both a brilliant and trusted woman in that company but she never got the title of vice president that she wanted and deserved.

Her thriftiness may have gotten the best of her. Her one extravagance was a mink coat that kept her warm on her commute from New Jersey. Other than that, she didn't dress in the Estee Lauder image and that may well have kept her from the very top tier.

Clothes for Work

If you adopt only one of the ideas in this book, make it this one. Wear clothes appropriate to the position you want in your company.

A few examples:

I once met young lady who worked in inside sales support at a real estate office. Then she moved to a more visible position in a bank. When we met for a consultation, she was had clean but stringy long hair and was wearing very large dangling earrings, an overblouse, dark jeans, and strapped shoes. All of this was very much in style but not for a bank employee. When she asked for advice, I suggested she either wear her hair in a more controlled style or get it cut. Other

1.1 Image Bearing

suggestions: Save the long dangling earrings for after work; wear pearls or button earrings. Always wear a jacket. No denim. Wear shoes that don't expose a lot of skin.

The next time I saw her, she had totally changed her appearance. And within six months of that change, she had a new job in the bank and a bigger paycheck.

Dressing Down

This is easy when you are in your home. You can do anything you want. But at a business event, even one that's casual, you still need to be aware of your image. You shouldn't wear a skimpy bikini to the corporate picnic, no matter how great your body is.

Remember: Casual Friday does not mean sloppy. Your clothes should fit well and be sharp and professional in appearance.

What gives you the image?

We were at a picnic following my nephew's baptism. My cousin Patty said to the minister, "Pastor! I

1.1 Image Bearing

didn't recognize you with your clothes on!" Without the visual cues, Patty had missed his identity.

When you wear the same style to work, you are being consistent. While I was working in a large insurance company, a new person was hired as assistant to the Director of Purchasing. As the door to the office opened, we jumped from behind our cubicle walls to see who was hired. What we saw was a very well-dressed woman. We decided that couldn't be the new hire. She was too well dressed to be an assistant to the purchasing agent.

She never changed her look. It was always professional, always like her boss. Two years later, she had her boss's job.

IT IS IMPORTANT THAT YOU BRAND YOURSELF.

Branding by appearance or behavior is so powerful that we have to be in control of it.

Your brand is the sum total of all the personal and public encounters with people who know you, your products, or your services, They will build your

1.1 Image Bearing

reputation and they will tell others about what it's like to work with you.

"If you don't brand yourself, you can rest assured that others are branding you. And letting others brand you can be risky business"

.... Tom Peters

The importance of being genuine.

We've talked about the importance of accentuating and camouflaging your appearance to project the personal image that you wish to project, We also need to explore the concept of being genuine.

Remember, even though you may be changing your behavior and your appearance, you're not becoming someone else.

. There are three reasons to be genuine.

- You want people to know that you are trustworthy, consistent, and dependable.

- You want to be known for your reputation, both physical and spiritual.

1.1 Image Bearing

- You want to be known as someone w... safe to do business with.

Trust and personal trustworthiness is a priceless commodity. Here's why -- when you are trustworthy, you get to be the keeper of secrets.

When you are keeper of secrets, you may get information from a number of sources who know that what they tell you will be kept in confidence. That information can give you a broader and clearer vision of your business community and business opportunities.

The importance of being consistent

Consistency is a necessary component of your brand because people want to be able to rely on your predictability.

Michele always came to work at 9:00 a.m. You could set the clock by her schedule. She would start the coffee pot, settle in at her desk, pick up any overnight messages from the phone and distribute them accordingly. She would be ready for a meeting to go over the day's work right after that.

I knew that if I came in at 7:30 and prepared the work I needed her do, we could meet at 9:30 to go over it. It was a joy to know that I could set my schedule by her schedule.

The importance of being dependable

Although dependability seems to be the same as consistency, it is not. Being consistent means you do the same thing the same way every time. Dependability means getting the job done within expectations. I can be dependable without being consistent.

Being dependable is just as important as consistency but it casts a wider net. You will develop repeat customers or clients because they can be sure of the quality of the product or service you offer.

Your first impression is often the information people receive when they first meet you.

1.1 Image Bearing

Who are you and how do others feel when they meet you? Do you prepare yourself before meetings and gatherings to be informed about current events? Do you know the latest news from the Wall Street Journal or Bloomberg's Business Week Magazine? Do people want to talk to you because you have information they would like to have? Do you use your knowledge as part of your branding?

Randi earns his living as a lawyer and commercial real estate manager. It is a very intense business. Randi also has a foundation that teaches yoga and other meditative techniques. His first impression is always soft, gentle, and understanding. He is a great listener and a gently probing communicator. He does not seem like a person who you would normally find in commercial real estate sales. He communicates his gentleness to his tenants. He also communicates resolve and tenacity as a spiritual leader. His spiritual reputation precedes him. As a result, he can solve problems with far less stress.

The importance of generosity and kindness.

Why would I want to be more generous and kind? Here are a few reasons you might want to consider.

1.1 Image Bearing

---

1. **Generosity Breeds Generosity.**

    Although it seems like a one way street, generosity actually moves in both directions.

    According to the Wall Street Journal, Rotary is the largest privately funded service organization in the world. In Rotary, I saw a request for financial aid to help recovery from a tsunami in Japan build to an $18,000 gift. It starts with one person and then another adds a few more dollars. As the effort is publicized, more people start writing checks and the gift grows.

2. **Generosity makes our spirit feel good.**

    For example: My husband signed us up to be the cleaning crew on a busy local thoroughfare as part of his Rotary Club's community service project. It was a Saturday morning early in the spring. We had said we would do it, but I wanted to stay home to do some work. (Commercial design firms always have last-minute projects; they would work 24/7 if they could.) On this particular Saturday, I needed to be in the office by 9:00 a.m. ready to finish a big project.

1.1 Image Bearing

We started as early as we could, to start the cleaning of this stretch of road. Our team was scheduled to start at 7:00 a.m., but Jerry and I started our portion of the road at 6:30. We walked the highway with trash bags, work gloves, and a poker that Jerry had made from a broom handle and a nail. I don't remember what we picked up, but I do remember that the experience was amazing. We walked, talked, and picked up trash. The sun was up but the fog had not quite burned off. The air was fresh, fragrant and refreshing. We talked about work, family, finances and us. We worked for about two hours, walking up one side of of the road and down the other.

It's been quite a few years since we did that. And yet I can still smell the fragrant air. We cleaned up trash but it felt like a more intense experience. We were alone, talking, laughing and sharing. The work in our office, the big project, seemed like a breeze when we got there at 8:45. We were refreshed and ready to go to work.

3. People will notice your generosity

1.1 Image Bearing

You will notice when people are generous. Really, you will notice. You'll see a person begging on the street and you'll smile when you see a passerby giving a dollar or a little change. You will notice when the kids stand in the middle of the street collecting for THON – a Pennsylvania State University Project that raises money for cancer research. The students collect money around the world for this project. And people will notice when *you* give, no matter how big the donation.

4. People will talk about your generosity in a positive way

"He/she is so generous." When people say that about you, they are speaking more about your attitude than your wallet or purse. You are providing them with good information about yourself. They like you or they wouldn't be talking about your generosity.

5. Generosity will enable you to breathe more easily.

When you give away some of your hard earned money, you begin to realize that there is more where that came from. You recognize that you are not destitute;

1.1 Image Bearing

you can breathe more easily about yourself and your life. And you can breathe more easily about your financial situation.

In the 1980's, as I walked through Grand Central Station, the homeless were huddled around the heating vents with blankets and what looked like fences made of cardboard. I walked through Grand Central at about 6:00 p.m., twice a month. For one of those trips, I decided to bring food. I was afraid as I thought about going up to these poor souls. I asked a male passerby if he would walk with me to distribute the fruit and vegetables. Thankfully, he agreed. We distributed the food quietly and quickly.

I have no idea what I thought would happen. Would I get yelled at for not giving them money? Or for not giving them a steak and lobster dinner? Would one person grab it all, leaving nothing for the rest? There was silence for the most part, a nod of a head, an occasional "thank you." I didn't leave there flying high at my meager donation. I left just being able to breathe.

Walking through the train station with bags of food was enriching. Walking out without the pounds of food I

1.1 Image Bearing

carried walking in lightened my body and my mind. I walked a little slower to my destination; my mind seemed to have a place to rest. I felt healthy. Yes, my mind and body liked the chance to give to others. It wasn't a spiritual thing but a physical acknowledgement of a caring act.

6. The Power of Truth

When people are not truthful with me, my reaction is to avoid them. If you lie, people will see right through you. There is something in your voice, your facial expression, or your body language that tips people off. They know when they are being manipulated and they don't like it. If they were asked how they knew someone was lying, they might answer, "It's just a feeling."

That said, you don't need to reveal everything. There is such a thing as privacy.

You are comfortable in your skin when you tell the truth, no matter what. This means that you have surrounded yourself with your own personal truths. You like who you are because you haven't lied to *yourself*.

1.1 Image Bearing

You have faced facts and taken responsibility for the outcomes in your life that you have created, both positive and negative.

You also tell the truth because you want people to trust you. Trust is what builds your relationships. It makes you more dependable.

7. Consistency is Constancy

We've been talking a lot about trust. When you are <u>consistent</u>, you develop a <u>level of trust</u>. Because you are consistent in your behavior, people expect specific outcomes from you. Those outcomes can be anything from delivering on time to having an organized base of knowledge.

Consistency will bring repeat customers by giving them a repeat experience. This is why franchises are successful. You can trust that you will have the same experience from a chain restaurant in New York as you will in California. As our society is becoming more and more mobile, we look for consistency in our day-to-day travels.

Consistent behavior is measurable.

1.1 Image Bearing

If you have to submit a proposal that is larger than you have attempted before, how do you know how to approach it? You need to accurately project how long it will take to complete and what the cost will be. Unless your behavior has been consistent and measurable, you won't be able to put a price tag on it.

But if you've been consistent in the past, you can put together a profitable, predictable proposal based on your past behavior. You may not be dead-on accurate. But chances are good you will have a reasonable, reliable, profitable proposal.

Consistency is your golden key. It supports you with a favorable impression in the workplace, in the community, and at home. Consistency becomes your reputation.

1.2 Conventions

Conventions
Customs and Etiquette

1.2 Conventions

"**Manners are a sensitive awareness of the feelings of others. If you have that awareness, you have good manners, no matter which fork you use.**"   ~Emily Post

1.2 Conventions

Conventions, Customs and Etiquette

"When in Rome, do as the Romans do." That advice also applies to you when you interact with high-level business people. You need to know the customs that govern their behavior. You'll get some tips in this chapter.

Why Business Dinner Etiquette?

Because if you don't know better you may eat someone else's food. *"Don't eat someone else's roll"* – this actually happened to me.

When I was growing up I never knew that people used more than a fork, a knife and a spoon to eat lunch or dinner. Those same three pieces were used daily. The first time I was at a dinner table where there were more than three pieces of flatware, I was fifteen years old. I had never seen a table set with one plate on top of another or set with more than one fork.

1.2 Conventions

I started to question my heritage. How could I not know about the formality of dining? After all, my father came from Scotland, which meant he was just one step away from Royalty. My Aunt Hannah owned commemorative china cups and saucers from Queen Elizabeth II's coronation. I thought we were insiders. Shouldn't I know, somehow, through my genes, all about table settings and etiquette?

Well maybe I should have known, but I didn't. In time, though, I learned about table settings.

What's the point? The point is that knowing about dinner-table etiquette helps you to promote a positive image for yourself and your company. How you perform at a business dinner reflects on who you are.

Is it important? Many colleges and universities think so. They are now adding courses in restaurant and public-event dining, as well as business etiquette, to their required courses for business majors.

When you have an 11:00 a.m. job interview, it may have been scheduled at that time because you seem like a potential good hire. If you do well in the interview, they may want to see how you behave in a professional but casual setting, so they invite you to

1.2 Conventions

lunch. Will you pass that test? Only if you're comfortable with dining etiquette.

That's where business etiquette comes in. Business etiquette not only increases your social currency, it also gets you more respect from your boss and from your clients.

Using correct dining etiquette when you eat in public also makes you more effective. You may find this comparison silly, but the knowledge you need to make an educated stock buy are the same as what you need to know to pass the mashed potatoes. Both require attention to detail, consideration of people, and knowledge of the situation.

Lack of attention to business etiquette could hurt your image and might even cost you your job.

And here's another thing to think about. Knowing business etiquette makes you confident. And confidence is what success is all about. When you know the rules of etiquette, you don't have to worry about how to act because it's part of who you are.

The more comfortable you are with dining with business associates, the more confidence your boss will have in

1.2 Conventions

your ability. And he/she your boss will breathe a sigh of relief because you'll be able to share the burden of entertaining dinner guests.

If you're comfortable with the rules and customs of a business dinner, you become a valuable commodity to your company. For that reason, your chances for promotions and raises increase the more fluent you are in business etiquette,

Knowing how to behave in a business setting not only increases your visibility, it also boosts management's opinion of your work ethic and productivity.

And the more events you attend, the more people have a chance to see how you handle yourself. When you do it well, you become the face of the company. People you meet outside your day-to-day work with your company are able to see how well you handle yourself.

So let's get down to the nuts and bolts of dinner-table etiquette.

First things first -- when you sit down, place your napkin on your lap, folded in half with the fold nearer your body.

1.2 Conventions

Next -- take a look at the table setting. It may seem intimidating, but it is logical.

FORMAL TABLE SETTING

1. Soup bowl
2. Appetizer or salad plate
3. Service plate
4. Water glass
5. White wine glass
6. Red wine glass
7. Napkin
8. Fish fork
9. Dinner fork
10. Salad fork
11. Service knife
12. Fish knife
13. Soup spoon
14. Bread and butter service
15. Dessert spoon
16. Dessert fork

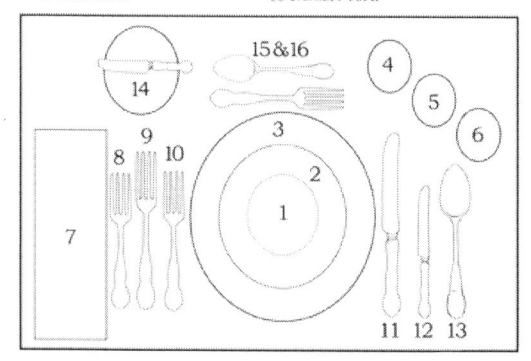

This picture shows what the setting may look like. You may not see all of these pieces, but the same general rule applies -- you use the utensils from the outside in, and when you run out, you use the ones on top.

It is easy to be confused when at a round table set for eight - everything is crammed together. Here's a way to make sure you don't eat someone else's roll. Just

1.2 Conventions

think of BMW – Bread, Main Meal and Water – left to right. Your bread is on your left, your water is on your right.

The dinner plate is the focal point. In some high-end restaurants, you don't eat off the plate that's in the center. It's for decoration and will either be removed or your dinner plate will go on top.

More on napkins. Use your napkin to blot your lips, if water, wine, or other liquid makes a break for it. Don't use it to blot lipstick or as a place to put food you find unacceptable. Take unwanted food out of your mouth with the same utensil you used to put it in. If the food went in with your fingers, take it out with your fingers. Set the food on the edge of your plate.

If you need to leave your seat, excuse yourself and put your napkin on the back of your chair. Where you place your napkin on the table can convey a message to the wait staff and a waiter will take a cue from where you put your napkin or flatware.

Here are some examples:

A napkin to the left of your plate usually means that you haven't arrived yet. A napkin to the right of your plate indicates you've left. A napkin on the arm of your

1.2 Conventions

chair or the back of your seat means you've left temporarily. Another hint: To keep food stains off the chair seat, don't put your napkin there.

Other signals for the waiter include leaving your knife and fork at 4 and 8 o'clock to signal that you are still eating. Utensils diagonally parallel indicate you are finished.

Bread always stays on the bread plate. When you butter your bread, never use butter from the common plate. Instead put some on your own bread plate and use that butter.

We didn't learn about passing food from my Uncle Harry. He always passed it both to the right and to the left just to see the collision when the mashed potatoes and turnips met in the middle. Not correct. Always pass food to the right.

The person who picks up a serving dish should offer it first to the person on their left **before** passing it to the right. If someone asks you to pass a serving plate, you should first pass it to the person who asked for it before you serve yourself.

Most business events feature a more informal place setting. In a menu where, salad, entrée, and dessert would be served, the setting would probably look like this.

INFORMAL TABLE SETTING

Dining etiquette isn't all about which fork to use, however. You weren't invited because you needed a hot meal. You need to be prepared to have a conversation.

It is polite to introduce yourself to everyone at the table. If you are at a business event, add your company name. You can also add a tag line, to explain who you are, why you have been invited to the event, or a description of your business. For example, "Hi I'm Linda, I'm Alan's first cousin," or "I'm Linda Reed Friedman with Advanta Strategies, a consulting firm."

1.2 Conventions

If the table has eight seats, you may want to walk around the table and introduce yourself. Shouting across the table is not proper etiquette.

How to get the conversation started? Here are the most commonly used questions. Most people have quick answers to these.

"Do you live around here?"

"How did you come to be at this event, birthday party, or wedding?"

"Tell me about your business."

"What is your favorite sport?"

"Do you play that sport or are you a spectator?"

"What's your favorite dessert?"

Here are some that require more thought:

"How does your typical day go?" (This can be fun when you ask an executive this.)

"What are you passionate about besides your business?"

"What book are you currently reading?"

"Tell me about it."

1.2 Conventions

Other Conversation Starters

Always read the morning newspaper. You can also go to a Web site like Mashable to find out what's trending in social media before you go to an event. Pick few non-controversial but interesting subjects to discuss.

If you read an overview of business best sellers, you can talk about the topics or points the authors make.

Ask the person next to you what his/her vision is for the next five years. Where does he/she see the world economy going? Tip: If you ask this kind of question, make sure you have a few answers yourself.

How to Handle a Mini-Disaster

Coughing or sneezing is usually a surprise. When we feel it coming on, however, the correct way to handle it is to put your face into your elbow. It may look funny to see someone look like they are whispering into the crook of their arm, but it's the most sanitary way to keep your germs to yourself. On the other hand, never blow your nose at the table. Excuse yourself from the table and then go wash your hands.

1.2 Conventions

The Thank-You Note

I've always hated to write thank-you notes. They seem so impersonal to me. Thank you for the blah-blah-blah I'll use it when I blah-blah-blah.

Actually, writing thank-you notes is really very simple. And it is very IMPORTANT.

When I send thank-you notes after business meetings to thank people for their suggestions, they remember me. And being remembered is an important key to your success.

Send your thank-you note out within a few days of the event; otherwise the person receiving it may not even remember you. Your thank-you note should mention any insights you got from your conversation, which will make it even more likely that you will be remembered.

A simple note is all you need. For example, you can say that you enjoyed getting to know the person better. You can also expand briefly on some of the topics you discussed. If your conversation was with an amateur cook, for example, you can offer some of your recipes. That kind of thoughtful response makes you remembered.

1.2 Conventions

A person's time is valuable. It pays to remember that time is a precious commodity and when it is gone, it is gone. So a thank-you note is called for when a person spends some of his/her time with you. Whether it's for a job interview or a networking contact, a thank-you note will also help boost your image.

If you travel for business, remember that saying thank-you is perfect in any language. When you visit other countries, learn to say thank-you in the native language.

Being a Power Professional Manager

Chapter 2.1 Leading Your Team

Leading your Team

Chapter 2.1 Leading Your Team

*"There is no **"I"** in team but there is in win."*
Michael Jordan

Chapter 2.1 Leading Your Team

Leading your Team

Teamwork

Everything I have learned about leadership and teamwork is the result of participating in organizations. When I rose to leadership roles in those organizations, it taught me important lessons about the value of teamwork and collaboration.

When I started my company, the LRF Design Group, I joined the International Facility Management Association (IFMA). Over the next several years, as my business and IFMA grew, so did my role in the organization and my understanding of the real meaning of teamwork.

I found that there are constant challenges when you are in business. Managing the activities of people in an organization is a daily task. At the LRF Design Group, we certainly made our share of mistakes but, in spite of it

Chapter 2.1 Leading Your Team

all, the company did not have to absorb a lot of losses, mostly because of teamwork.

A good example of teamwork is customer service. You may know what customer service means to you, but what I learned as a business owner that you cannot do it alone. You need a team of people working with you to help create a worthwhile customer service program.

I also found out that being in business gives you the opportunity to make lemonade every day. It is never IF the lemons will arrive, it's WHEN.

Let me share a few lemonade stories with you. **Lemonade Story # 1 -** In my first year in business, I was on fire. According to a Wall Street Journal article, only 5% of entrepreneurs had a gross business income of over $100,000 in 1983. I was one of the 5%.

The majority of my business came from one major corporation. My contact was a family friend who was an executive with the company. When he was swept out during a battle for control of the company, I got caught in the cross-fire. As a result, I lost a substantial part of my business.

Chapter 2.1 Leading Your Team

Looking back, I see that as the catalyst that led me to create a larger, more productive company for myself. I had to get business and I learned how. I was forced to push myself in new ways and that turned out to be a good thing.

Lemonade Story #2 – At the height of a very busy time, I lost half of my employees. We had employees with babies being born, people moving away, and some people leaving because they didn't get the promotion they expected. We also trained our people very well and a few large design firms used us as a recruiting source to grow their company.

It all just happened at once and it was a demoralizing experience for me. And yet, even with so many of my team gone, the following year was more profitable than the year before. The key was good, solid customer service.

I'd like to show you how -- through customer service, teamwork, and collaboration -- it all happened for us.

I have six simple tips:

Chapter 2.1 Leading Your Team

1. Smile

A single encounter can establish a customer's perception of the overall service of an organization. Your customers have mental notebooks in which they record every action and transaction. At some point, there is a moment of truth that sets the entire tone of the customer's relationship with you. That moment should be accompanied by a chuckle. SMILE! Here are some ways to generate the smiles.

Slow down - Smiling will slow you down and help you listen. Take notes. This attention to detail helps the client know they have been heard. Ask questions. Lots of questions.

It's easy to smile, so do it often. When you are on the phone or meeting someone for the first time, smile. It conveys an attitude. It tells those you meet that you are strong and capable. They will know you are up to the challenges of the day and your life. They will know that you have a willingness to do the job they need done.

Chapter 2.1 Leading Your Team

After we moved to Pennsylvania, I got my real estate license and worked with a man named Chuck Gambone. He *always* smiled and whenever a glitch came up, he would say, "Not a problem," and then go and fix it. It was his problem not yours.

In fact, Chuck and I like the same author, Og Mandino. When I first read his book "The Greatest Secret in the World", I thought it was self-help book about being a better salesperson. A few years later I picked it up and read it again. I found that it wasn't about salesmanship, it was about *attitude*. It's really a basic textbook on how to behave and how to change your thinking. .

My attitude changed early on after reading Og Mandino's book. I was working for Blue Cross and Blue Shield of New Jersey and I had the prestigious title of Construction Communication Coordinator, which really meant that I had lots of responsibility and no authority. Some of you may have even more prestigious titles and be in the same situation.

As part of my job, I was coordinating about a million square feet of space -- a big challenge. If staff

Chapter 2.1 Leading Your Team

members or a department were moving, they had my phone number – and they used it.

My attitude was heading into the dumpster. The phone was ringing off the hook with a never-ending list of job orders with cranky people. "Can't these people ever be happy?" I asked myself.

I picked up Mandino's book, which told me that I could change my situation if I followed his suggestions. Obviously, one was to smile. He advised me to keep these words in mind --"I will laugh at the world." He also told me to laugh at myself, "for man is most comical when he takes himself too seriously."

I read the whole book many times. It was upbeat and positive. I smiled more. When someone asked "How are you doing? My answers suddenly became "Terrific," "Fabulous," and "Wonderful."

You may think this positive attitude stuff is a bunch of hooey. But let's talk about results.

My smiling and positive attitude was well received but, my job got worse. People thought they could talk to me now because I was nice. They called more often with

Chapter 2.1 Leading Your Team

their complaints, so I decided to think of them not as complaints but challenges to solve.

The thing about working in facilities management is that no one really knows what you do until it's not being done. This is especially true if you're doing such an outstanding job that it appears effortless. The more the projects move along easily the less you are recognized. You are always in danger of being taken for granted.

But my positive attitude actually made me more visible in the company. The visibility created an opportunity for me to work with my boss's boss's boss, a top-tier senior executive. And as a result of more visibility and my attitude change, my performance reviews got better. In less than a year, my salary increased by 25% and my title was changed from coordinator to manager.

There was also a very subtle change that made a huge difference in my job. People began to think I cared about them and they started to be proactive. I found that maintenance issues got to me before they became catastrophic. When you take care of the little stuff, the

Chapter 2.1 Leading Your Team

big stuff doesn't get up a head of steam and blow up. It's better to be warned about a wobbly chair than to have someone out on disability with a back problem.

It all started with the smile, a chuckle, and a behavior change.

In business, I want the opportunity to provide service to also be an opportunity to smile. Do you want to be perceived as being willing? Smile.

That also means we have to behave as if we are willing.

We need to treat our team members with the same smile, the same upbeat positive attitude, and remember they are stakeholders as well.

Who are these people? They are our employees, our friends, our colleagues. our customers, our superiors, our suppliers.

Change your behavior, change your attitude. If all else fails, "FAKE IT TILL YOU MAKE IT." Besides, the smile is free and it doesn't hurt.

2. Be helpful.

Chapter 2.1 Leading Your Team

How do you build strong relationships? You become helpful without being asked. The most effective way of doing that is to fill a need that you observe, not one you are told about.

Do you fully understand your customers' expectations? And do your customers fully understand your capabilities, not just from your company's product line but from your greater presence in the marketplace and the world? A customer's expectations go beyond the product and service. Their expectations include how information is delivered, or how billing is done, or how problems are solved.

But there are times our clients aren't sure of what they need. That's when we need to be helpful and build a relationship of trust and confidence. The feeling of trust and confidence or lack of it can make or break the relationship.

When I first started my business, I was a very small design firm. I was working with about six people out of my basement. To get to my backwoods house, you turned onto a dirt road and up a dirt driveway and

Chapter 2.1 Leading Your Team

you were at the World Headquarters for the LRF Design Group.

When I was working with a client, I would always recommend Herman Miller products. Tim, a salesperson from Steelcase, a competitor of Herman Miller, realized that I needed more education.

Tim took me on a tour of Steelcase with other designers from much larger companies. He was helping me get educated but he was also helping me see my company as a much larger entity than I was and worthy of his investment of time and resources.

As a result of his interest, I recommended a new product he showed me for a small research facility we were designing for Exxon. None of the Steelcase dealers on the East Coast had been able to land the Exxon account and my recommendation of a cutting-edge product from Steelcase helped open the door for them and gave them a huge opportunity. A win-win.

3. Be Aware

Chapter 2.1 Leading Your Team

Be aware of your surroundings – of your environment. Be especially aware for clues about your clients.

Be observing small things, like how your clients decorate their office space or how they dress, you can get a good idea of what they are like. In the same way, knowing what kind of restaurants they like or how they treat others when they talk on the phone can give you valuable information.

The office layout and furnishings can also tell you a lot. I once walked out of a dentist's office because I could tell that his office furniture was expensive. That told me that his fees were most likely more than I wanted to spend. On the other hand, if I were going to a plastic surgeon, I'd look his or her office differently. I would want it to look good but not too expensive, with everything done in good taste and well kept.

When you shake hands with a client, you often can a glue to her personality. A firm handshake says something different than a limp one.

Chapter 2.1 Leading Your Team

4. Listen

Listening is the first step in finding out what your customer needs. Listening to the customer talk about what they need and hearing those needs is the key to knowing what's really on their minds.

First rule: Don't interrupt with a proposed solution until they finish. Doing that tends to shut people off and you will lose a chance to learn. What you are really telling them is that your mind is made up. Additionally, your answers, solutions, or conclusions may not be accurate.

When you are listening, it's helpful to know the difference between empathy and sympathy. When you are sympathetic to your client, you take on their problems and concerns. You can end up on an emotional rollercoaster, which can derail the best of plans.

When you are empathetic you have a chance to stand back and acknowledge the problem with minimal emotional involvement. Your response could be: "I can understand how that makes you angry." The trick is to be emotionally sensitive without being involved. When

Chapter 2.1 Leading Your Team

you respond with empathy, you stay calm and in control. That's when you are at your best.

The kind of listening I'm talking about is like a quiet conversation over lunch. It's hearing the frustration in someone's voice and asking questions. "Gee, I hear you. What's that all about?"

Listening is not my strength. I get very quick and accurate information from my stomach. Sometimes my reactions shift from empathy to sympathy to anger. And then I tend to say what I feel. In fact, I have cuts and bruises on my lips from trying to keep my mouth shut. And I'm really embarrassed when a different me emerges from my mouth and my ears slam shut.

Here's an example. Back in the early 80's, a facility manager in a building I was working on complained about having to make specific appointments with me. He said it would be more helpful if he could have one of my designers/project managers on-site at his facility for a couple of weeks.

I heard him but I didn't want to listen because I'm a control freak. My mind came up with lots of reasons why this wasn't a good idea. I didn't want my company

Chapter 2.1 Leading Your Team

to be judged by the quality of an unsupervised, new-to-the-field designer. If one of my designers was working on-site, I might lose some level of control. I might not be able to keep watch on the quality of the service and the products we were putting out.

Eventually, though, I did listen and we negotiated a deal that included my supervision. The outcome of listening to this client was the beginning of outsourcing for my company, which became a strong foundation for my business. My designer worked for years at this company and, in time, other members of my staff also worked there as the number of the company's projects ebbed and flowed.

We learned to listen and in time it became a natural thing to do.

Another way we listened that was critical to our success was to write "meeting minutes" during phone calls. Most times they were scribbled; sometimes they were legible. But you can tell a lot from quickly written words and scribbled handwriting.

It got so we could make judgments about the phone call from how the notes are written – the size of

Chapter 2.1 Leading Your Team

the writing and even the writing implement that was used. When an assistant left me notes on a phone call, I could tell the attitude of my client just by looking at the note pad. When I called the next day, I could be clear because the notes were fresh.

You also need to listen to more than just the details of a specific project. You should also ask questions about the bigger picture of the client's business. Ask about their lives and always ask open-ended questions that can be followed up with "Tell me more." With these nuggets of information, you can understand their issues better and hear opportunities.

5. **Be Ethical**

Ethics is hard to define, but in 1932, Herb Taylor, a Chicago Rotarian, came up with these 24 words that put the definition into a nutshell.

"Of the things we think, say, or do....

Is it the truth?

Is it fair to all concerned?

Will it build good will and better friendships?

Will it be beneficial to all concerned?"

Chapter 2.1 Leading Your Team

Rotarians call this the Four-Way Test and it's a powerful tool to build relationships and trust.

Ethics is the foundation of a successful team. Add other ingredients like defined roles and responsibilities and you have a team built on trust and respect.

Ethics should be at the heart of your business. What is your mission statement? Mine is to help businesses and people through a process of "learn, act, and grow." Notice that the mission is focused not on me, but on the customer. This doesn't happen by accident, but by design.

Does ethical behavior produce results? Taylor wrote his definition of ethics for his company, Club Aluminum, which was heading into bankruptcy. He knew that to save his business, he needed an ethical yardstick that everybody in the company could memorize and apply to what they said and did in their dealings with others.

He used this yardstick in his relationships with vendors and customers alike, even when being fair might cost his company more money. In five years, Club

Chapter 2.1 Leading Your Team

Aluminum had pulled itself out of the red using Taylor's test.

6. Be Trustworthy

We are a very interdependent society. We need to work with each other to succeed. To do that, we need to trust each other. And trust is built through face-to-face interaction.

Trust begins with being trustworthy. You can't build trust with others if you don't behave in a trustworthy manner.

It's easier to build trust if you subscribe to some core beliefs about mankind in general that lead to unity and goodwill rather than separateness and suspicion. You need to see other people as allies in the journey of life rather than as adversaries.

If you can see others as being on your side instead of against you, it will be easier to be honest with them and build a relationship based on mutual trust.

Chapter 2.1 Leading Your Team

Simple Leadership Tips

Chapter 2.2 -   More Simple Leadership Tips

"A good leader takes a little more than his share of the blame, a little less than his share of the credit" …… **Arnold H. Glasow**

Chapter 2.2 -   More Simple Leadership Tips

Simple Leadership Tips

Ask for Help

What does a leader do? A leader asks for help. Asking for help can be the beginning of a valuable relationship.

When you ask for help you begin to create a group of people who will support you. Some people will be better than others at responding, but that doesn't really matter. It's the support, the camaraderie, and the creation of a functional team that should be your goal.

People enjoy helping. You can find one example of that in the subways of New York City. The New York subway map looks like a bowl of spaghetti and is hard to figure out. If you need help to find your way, just stand next to the map and look confused or ask a passerby for help. A New Yorker will offer you at least three ways to get to your destination. Other passersby, overhearing your conversation, will chime in. Soon there will be a

Chapter 2.2 - More Simple Leadership Tips

crowd of people with strong opinions about the best way to get from A to B.

Lesson: Asking for help usually yields a positive response and often results in several solutions to a problem.

You begin building a supportive team by asking someone to help you accomplish a task. Even if it would take you less time if you did it yourself, your dual objectives are solving a problem <u>and</u> making a connection. The first task can be a simple one, like producing and distributing the minutes of a meeting. You can follow that with a larger task like producing the monthly newsletter.

To get a positive response to your request you need to be very specific. Whether you are dealing with a volunteer or a paid employee, the rules are the same. First describe your desired result and then talk about the specific tasks that need to be done and the time frame in which it needs to be accomplished.

If you are clear and specific when you talk about the task, you give the person you ask the energy to bring to the job. They can be creative and proud of the work they do because they know exactly what you expect.

Chapter 2.2 -   More Simple Leadership Tips

Say "Thank you"

When you get help, it's important to say "Thank You". People will never get tired of hearing you say "thank you". They may even say, "Stop it, you've already said "thank you." But don't stop. Saying "thank you" is an essential ingredient in being a good leader.

Ask for feedback.

It always helps to ask for feedback. " How can we do what we do better?" "What should we not be doing?" "What should we be doing that we aren't doing?"
Asking these questions will encourage an increased level of support.

Ask for ideas.

Asking for ideas is an excellent team-building tactic. But you must make sure you create an action plan to use the ideas you get. Because those ideas are precious. You are being given a gift and you must show you appreciate the gift.

Chapter 2.2 -   More Simple Leadership Tips

A friend of mine is an executive director of a very large non-profit that distributes huge sums of money into the community. The members of her board of directors are brilliant and engaged in her organization's work, with lots of ideas. Her rule is to thank them for their contributions and ask them to flesh out put their ideas with as much information.

You should always acknowledge a person's contribution and thank them. You don't need to drop balloons from the ceiling, blow horns, and sprinkle confetti around – a simple "thank you" will do. If it's too expensive in time and money to implement their ideas, however, you should explain that you may not be able to act on their ideas immediately. Be sure to mention that you would like to receive more ideas.

BE A NURTURING CHEERLEADER

When nothing goes according to plan, and "Murphy's Law" has shown up to sidetrack a project, a successful leader needs to be nurturing and supportive. When things aren't going well, resist the temptation to

Chapter 2.2 -   More Simple Leadership Tips

look for people to blame. Instead, be sensitive to yourself and to the people who are supporting you.

Be gentle, be understanding, be diplomatic, and be authoritative. But don't be superior. There is no reason to give anyone a guilt trip.

Be a nurturing cheerleader!

What does it take to do that? It doesn't take much effort but you do need a very positive, supportive attitude.

Again. You say "thank You" for everything. Even if they are your paid employee, you say thank you. In reality, your employees are volunteers. They don't have to work for you. They are working for the money. They can volunteer at another job where they earn money.

People work for you because they want to. And they want to be appreciated for their contribution, no matter how small.

When you compliment an employee for doing a good job, use their name. Say "good job" <u>with their name</u>.

Chapter 2.2 -   More Simple Leadership Tips

Give Rewards

When my husband was in charge of the annual Rotary Pancake Breakfast, there was one volunteer who took care of the cooking, which meant pancakes for about 200 people. Plus being there Friday night to set up and spending all of Saturday morning cooking over a hot stove.

How do you reward that kind of effort? My husband painted a spatula with gold paint, mounted it on an award base and presented this person the "Golden Spatula" award for outstanding effort. It cost very little, but the value of the appreciation was priceless.

The manager of our local radio station had a lamp in the shape of a light bulb in his office. When I asked about it, he said it was an award for helping to run an on-air contest. "Because I was the host, I had to be in the studio each morning with one of our contestants who had to come into the studio each morning. Then, I had to run out of the studio, conduct the morning sales meeting, and then go back into the studio to finish up the contest. Because of that effort that I put in, I got this award."

Chapter 2.2 - More Simple Leadership Tips

A few more ways to recognize employees:

Compliment people to other people. To Suzy you might say, "Joe did a great job on that installation." It will get back to Joe. Suzy will tell.

Write compliments on post-it notes and put them it on a staff member's computer. That way, everyone will get to see the note.

Taking the time to write a thank-you note is one of the best tributes. Thank you for your time, thank you for finding the information I needed. It is a small gesture but it makes a big impression.

Give out stars - Give out stars to people who have shown special effort in completing a task. Give out stars when you observe people helping other people.

When a carpet installer arrived on one of my job sites, I looked at the space and saw that almost none of the rooms was square, which meant it was going to be a challenging installation. It was; it took him all day to do it. He carpeted 4.000 square feet of space and only complained a little. After I signed the usual form, I put a star on it.

I also said that it was an interesting installation and something he could talk about back at the office. He

Chapter 2.2 -   More Simple Leadership Tips

said the only thing he would share about the installation was the star I gave him. He left absolutely beaming.

For more ideas, read "How to Reward Employees" by Bob Nelson. It's a first-rate source of ways to recognize the efforts of your employees or volunteers in your organization.

Keep Your Cool

I have had a really hard time learning to think before I speak. When a conversation becomes intense and the interaction is lively, or when opinions are being offered that run counter to my own opinions, I want to speak up.

When I find myself confronted with disappointing news, a lack of support for my ideas, or any challenge to my way of thinking, my first instinct is to speak up, loudly.

I was at a meeting when the conversation turned to a project I was hoping to win. The submission deadline was that day and I had just submitted my proposal. During the conversation, I found out that

Chapter 2.2 -   More Simple Leadership Tips

another firm had already been awarded the project a few days earlier.

    I was not only disappointed, but I was furious hearing that the contract had been awarded before the submission deadline. I expressed my disappointment forcefully to everyone at the table.

    I'll never know what the impact of that behavior was on my personal and business life. Over time, however, I've learned the best way to handle situations like that is to bite your tongue, take a breath, and, if necessary, walk away.

    If you are alone, when you hear disappointing news and when your mind starts to run negative scenarios, a useful tool is to say, "Be quiet" out loud. When your mind hears your voice saying "Be quiet," it listens.

Be understood and understand

    When you think you're about to lose your cool, try repeating what the other person said back to them. That does two things -- the person you are talking with knows that you have heard them and they also have a chance

Chapter 2.2 - More Simple Leadership Tips

to correct you, if you didn't hear what was said exactly. This creates a more productive interaction.

You can also turn this tactic around. To make sure the person you are speaking with understands you, ask them to summarize what you've said. That will help make sure you both are the same page. You still might not agree but you can verify that you both clearly understand the issues. And you now have the chance to change your words or your position, if it's appropriate.

This technique can be a bit unsettling. Once, when a client at a large pharmaceutical company asked me to repeat what he was asking me to design, I assumed that he thought I was stupid.

As the conversation progressed, however, I realized he wanted to confirm that I had an understood the design criteria and the work he wanted me to complete. That changed my attitude.

Once I learned this lesson, it changed the way I communicated with my clients. It made for more candid, efficient, and accurate communication.

Asking open-ended questions can also foster clearer communications. Try questions like "Can you tell

Chapter 2.2 - More Simple Leadership Tips

me more?", "How do you feel about that?", and "What do you think?"

Open- ended questions, give the person an opportunity to express themselves and perhaps also vent any frustration or anger they may be feeling.

"Tell me more" is an incredibly useful statement. I have a friend who uses those words frequently with her children. "Tell me more" lets her get emotion-free responses from her kids and her friends.

When someone asks you to tell them more, you often start to expand on what you said initially, even if you didn't think there was more to share. Even though the question is simple, and can be exceptionally encouraging. It helps a person tell you exactly how he thinks or feels.

Make it Fun - Surprise them with humor:

As a leader, encourage people to bring fun and humor to the job and the organization.

According to Aristotle "The secret to humor is surprise."

For example:

During pre-flight instruction, one Southwest Airlines pilot welcomes everyone aboard with references

Chapter 2.2 -   More Simple Leadership Tips

to Star Wars characters: "I'd love to introduce you to our flight attendants this evening, but they were put on a different flight – so we have C – 3PO and Chewbacca.". Occasionally Herb Kelleher, the former CEO of Southwest Airlines, would dress up in drag or as Elvis and visits the late night baggage handling crew. You can find pictures of Herb in a tutu or as Elvis sprinkled about the internet. Herb believed in a fun culture and gave it his support. The airline's record of success shows that he was doing something right.

Having fun takes some planning. For instance, when you plan a team meeting to discuss business issues, make it special. Add a surprise.

You don't need a reason to have fun. Every once in a while, take a time-out from your work and do something different. Buy everyone in the office an ice cream cone or take a walk around the block.

Contests and games are good ways to have fun. They can also help boost productivity while you're having fun.

Chapter 2.3 The Control is in Time Management

The Control is in Time Management

Chapter 2.3 The Control is in Time Management

> *"If we take care of the minutes, the years will take care of themselves."*
> ………………………..…...…..Benjamin Franklin

Chapter 2.3 The Control is in Time Management

Three Points about Time and Time Management

1. If you do not use it, you will lose it.
2. You cannot multi-task.
3. There is more than one way to manage your time.

1. If you don't use it, you'll lose it!

Time is not a commodity you can put on the shelf to get back later.

We all have the same 24 hours. Those 24 hours are priceless. We can use them or squander them. Use them wisely.

"Time is the scarcest resource, and unless it is managed, nothing else can be managed."

....Peter Drucker

2. You cannot multi-task.

According to recent research, multi-tasking can reduce productivity by approximately 40 percent.

Chapter 2.3 The Control is in Time Management

Switching from one task to another makes it difficult to tune out distractions and can cause mental blocks that can slow down your progress.

Kristen Hanahan, -- a realtor, Girl Scout leader, Toastmaster, and mother to active children – decided to stop multitasking in a focused, intensive way for two weeks. Here is what she said about her experience:

"Multi-tasking may work for some people but not everyone. I didn't document if I saved time or not, but there was one very clear outcome for me. I stopped being nervous, I felt calmer and I was able to make focused decisions."

Her comments were an eye opener for me. I thought I was saving time when I was multi-tasking, but I never considered the possibility I was creating more stress in my life.

3. There is more than one way to manage your time.

Here are a few:
The Ivy Lee Formula

Chapter 2.3 The Control is in Time Management

This classic story has been told many times. Ivy Lee was well known for his skills and talents in the field of public relations. Charles Schwab, the president of Bethlehem Steel, invited Lee to his office to speak to the company's sales managers because Schwab thought they were not being as productive as they could be.

When Schwab asked Lee how much he charged, he answered, "Nothing, if it does not work. If it does, pay me what it is worth to you."

The Ivy Lee System was so successful, Schwab thought that it was worth $25,000. That was in almost 100 years ago. In today's money, it would be worth almost $600,000.

What was Lee's formula? Lee requested a private meeting with each of the managers. What he said was this:

Before you leave your office or have decided that your work is done for the day, make a list of what you need to do tomorrow. In a random fashion, write down six items that need to be done. Then go back and prioritize them.

Chapter 2.3 The Control is in Time Management

The next day, start with the first item, complete it, and move on the next. Don't skip tasks. Start with the first task and go down the list in order.

The result was that the managers focused on completing each job before moving on and became more effective.

Give yourself the gift of time by scheduling your work

.

"Work expands so as to fill the time available for its completion."

....Cyril Northcote Parkinson – 1955

How true these words are. Here are a few ideas for timing yourself:

The best way to control the amount of time you spend on a job is to know how to create an accurate estimate of the time needed to do the job.

When we set a time limit this way, we tend to get it done. We stay focused and finish what we start.

Chapter 2.3 The Control is in Time Management

Timing yourself is everything, whether cleaning the bathroom or earning an academic degree.

Tracking your hours will also help you figure out how much time it will take to do the same type of project next time. Then you will be able to make a time estimate with confidence.

That said, I'm going to throw in a little caveat. A professor from DeSales University in Allentown, PA, speaking at a Project Management Institute event, said that most project estimates, whether they are done by an optimist or a pessimist, are almost always 20 to 40 percent over budget in time and money.

So when you are scheduling yourself and giving yourself a time limit, first estimate the time you'll need using your personal experience as a guide. Then multiply that number by 6 and divide it by 4.

Accurate time estimates can help prevent overtime, which is not only expensive but also can result in loss of cognitive function and an inability to schedule and prioritize tasks. Overtime also increases the likelihood of on-the-job accidents.

Chapter 2.3 The Control is in Time Management

Personally, I prefer using the "time limit method" for small tasks. However, if you use the "time limit method" for a big project, divide the project into smaller tasks and give those tasks individual time allocations.

For the larger projects, project management software can be invaluable in planning and tracking your time. It helps me to maintain my objectivity and to keep from losing money and disappointing clients.

Get yourself organized

Let's define "getting organized." I love a clean desk but that does not mean I'm organized. It just means I have a clean desk.

Organization means you are able to work efficiently without wasting time looking for background materials. It doesn't start and stop with your desk.

Your goal should be the ability to find something you are looking for within 60 seconds. That means you have to get rid of any stuff that gets in the way of meeting that objective.

Chapter 2.3 The Control is in Time Management

Note: When you make a date to clean out your desk, include the contents of your car.

In my first career, I taught art to the 7, 8 and 9th graders in three separate schools. With no supply storage available in the classrooms, my car became my art supply closet. As my trunk filled, the materials moved to the back seat of my car.

My art classes covered everything from Plaster of Paris for casting to zoological examples of colored egg shells for a mosaic art class. I had a slide projector for lectures, projects completed for grading and everything in between.

Although tall, I never played basketball. But in addition to my new position as an art teacher I was named the basketball coach. As my first year continued, material levels in the back seat of my car were almost at the level of the back of my front seat. One afternoon, after a long day – two schools and basketball practice, I began the drive home. Suddenly, two of my basketball/art students jumped up. They had hidden themselves in the backseat of my car under the piles of

Chapter 2.3 The Control is in Time Management

papers and materials. Organization would have gone a long way to preventing that.

A few organization tips for you to consider:

Begin by using a tracking system. When you put things down on paper, you remove the burden of remembering them from your mind. Write everything you need to do on a list. Use several pages to do this if you need them. When you finish a task cross it off.

One of the strongest tools in time management is file organization. Most of us use an alphabetical filing system. Each file folder has a letter of the alphabet, A through Z, and documents are filed by company name or client name.

A tickler file can also be very helpful. Keep a second filing drawer with 31 folders for the days of the month, and 12 folders for the months of the year. On any given day, you can pull reminders for that day from the appropriate folder. If you need to follow up at a later date, you can refile in the appropriate folder. Of course, today, in many electronic gadgets, there's an app for that.

Chapter 2.3 The Control is in Time Management

Overloaded files are a barrier to finding things easily, so you also need to keep your files up-to-date. Forty percent of the documents in them are likely to be obsolete or unnecessary. Even if you have switched to electronic files, you still need to clean out the debris.

Here's an example. My company, The LRF Design Group, specialized in corporate design work. On one large project we did, we facilitated the relocation of a large pharmaceutical company. Space was tight, and the president of the company was reluctant to order more file cabinets.

As one department was cleaning out files, they discovered six, four-drawer lateral files, 48" wide, that weren't being claimed by anyone. That was 96 linear feet of storage! And apparently the person who used those files had died five years before.

The president was right. In the process of cleaning out their personal spaces and unclaimed file drawers, additional filing space became available for everyone.

Organization can improve the quality of your work

Chapter 2.3 The Control is in Time Management

Getting yourself organized provides immediate benefits in terms of improving the quality of your work. Organization helps you think more clearly and you feel better with everything in its place.

But to maintain those benefits you have to keep yourself organized. I think this is harder than getting organized because putting everything back in its place every night is hard work. That is when routine and the good habits you've put in place should take over.

Negotiation

Chapter 2.4 Negotiate

Negotiations

"Let us never negotiate out of fear. But let us never fear to negotiate." ……………………..**John F. Kennedy**

Chapter 2.4 Negotiate

Preparing for a Successful Negotiation

Picture this. You and several others are leaving a crowded conference room, where you've spent the last three days. Most of the people leaving this hazy, hot, and humid atmosphere look worn out and disheveled. Not you.

Your boss is standing outside the room. He has a questioning look on his face.

You smile calmly. There is an air of confidence about you. Your blouse is crisp, your skirt is without a wrinkle and your shoes are sparkling.

You nod to our boss and say, "Yes." You are on top of your game.

At lunch you can tell your boss that, yes, you've been able to negotiate this complex, multilevel agreement. It supports your company's limited budget and aggressive time frame while making sure the project is also green.

Chapter 2.4 Negotiate

Your boss is nodding. He's smiling and he's saying, "Wow!" and "Good job!" as you share the details. You are clearly the expert here and it is an awesome feeling.

At home that night you brag about your negotiating skills. You tell your family that the negotiators on the other side said, "Are you crazy? Don't you want our business?" Then you said, "No, I don't want your business. Not with these numbers; they aren't working for me. How do we change that?"

You've got a major victory under your belt. What was your secret? You were well prepared.

3 Keys to Preparing for a Successful Negotiation

1. Be organized.
    - Research the situation.
    - Gather your resources.
    - Know the people you'll be facing at the negotiating table.
    - Prepare yourself for success.
2. Level the playing field.

Chapter 2.4 Negotiate

3. When it's time to negotiate, give yourself a little confidence-building self-talk.

1. Be Organized.

Research the situation thoroughly, gather the resources you will need, such as consultants and experts in your organization, know the people you will be facing in the negotiation, and prepare yourself for success

2. Research the situation –
   - The operations of the company or organization you will be negotiating with
   - Their strengths and weaknesses.
   - Products or services they produce
   - Organizational structure
   - Financial position
   - Look at your own organization.` Can you produce the product or service that is being requested? If not, what does your company need to do?
   - Is the time frame realistic?
   - Do you have the manpower?

Chapter 2.4 Negotiate

- Gather your resources --
  - A lawyer
  - A mediator
  - An accountant
  - A financial analyst
  - Relevant people in your organization

- Organize your materials. Organize your files alphabetically, so you can retrieve information quickly. Facts like the client's business background, company background, history. labor relations, personnel, and project specifications should be easy to find Your writing should be easily legible on each file or use tabs in 14 pt. type file folder

- Know the people with whom you will be negotiating --

- Find out who the leader is, and who controls the finances. Prepare yourself well

Chapter 2.4 Negotiate

enough so you to know exactly who you are going to be dealing with.

- Be prepared to make your points briefly, concisely and clearly. Simplicity is a key point.

- Researching your adversary also means seeing things through their eyes. What does your adversary really need, besides the list of wants he's negotiating for? What does he want intellectually and emotionally? Remember -- although he's your adversary, you still want to get on his good side.

- Don't make assumptions about what your adversary really wants. MGM studio Chief Samuel Goldwyn once tried to buy the film rights to several of George Bernard Shaw's plays. After protracted bargaining over the terms, Shaw decided not to sell. "The trouble is, Mr. Goldwyn"

Chapter 2.4 Negotiate

he said, "you are interested only in art and I am interested only in money." Goldwyn assumed Shaw was interested in making an artistic movie, but what Shaw really wanted was to make money on the deal. He didn't care about an artistic film.

When dealing with those on the other side of the negotiating table, you would like to make them reasonably happy with the outcome, so prepare yourself by knowing how to do that. But remember -- while it's important to know what makes your adversary happy, you shouldn't back off your objectives.

Sometimes, it's impossible for both sides to be satisfied with the results. If that happens, remember that your aim is to achieve your key bargaining goals. You can compromise, but don't back down on your key goals just to please your adversary. That is a lose-lose outcome. You want your negotiations to be a win-win.

Your attitude is another area where you need to be prepared. This is about your attitude going in. You must believe deep down inside that you are going to win – that your team has done an excellent job of

Chapter 2.4 Negotiate

preparation. And you need to believe that you won't stop short of the objectives you laid out before you started your negotiations.

Look inside yourself -- is there anything keeping you from a winning attitude? Do you have any doubts? Are you afraid? You need to deal with these attitudes to build up your confidence. How to do that? Be fully prepared -- learn everything you can about the people you will be negotiating with.

To help develop a winning attitude, research your facts and study them. Study the facts thoroughly – and then more than thoroughly. Study the facts so thoroughly that you believe 100% in your position.

You should also have the facts set in your mind. Not only should they be on paper, but you should also have them memorized at least well enough so that if you flip open your file you won't have to read it. You'll know the facts and you'll also know that with those facts at your command you can be successful.

Arming yourself with the facts gives you a positive attitude and your bearing will show it. Your posture will be straight, your back strong, your head will be held high

Chapter 2.4 Negotiate

– all because you've done your homework and you know that you are going to win.

Gather support. You can't always go into negotiations by yourself. When you start researching what the negotiation is about, you may decide that you need help from other people -- people who know more about specific issues then you do.

You can overcome any lack of knowledge at the negotiating table if you have someone with you who can help show you what the bargaining chips are and walk you through the maze your adversary is setting up for you.

You might need an attorney, for example, because there are points of law that are specific to the negotiation that he knows and you don't.

3. Level the Playing Field

Being a professional means acting like one. How do you do that? Part of your preparation is to anticipate your adversary's reaction to your proposals. You need to get inside his or her mind. To start, write a list of

Chapter 2.4 Negotiate

questions or points your adversary might make. Once you have the list, answer the questions in writing. Basically, you are writing your own script. For instance, "What should I say here if he asks for that? What should I say if she says this?" You need to mentally act out the entire negotiation, addressing all your "what ifs."

Role play is another strong tool. Have a colleague ask you the tough questions so you can rehearse the answers out loud.

As you work through different the possibilities, you'll begin to get a good handle on exactly what will happen during your meeting. You'll be knowledgeable and prepared. And it's all about preparation.

When you've done your homework, you become an expert and you know the answers. You can anticipate what will happen.

As strong as your position may be, however, you need to treat every person with respect. You do that by addressing every concern they have, whether you think it's important or not.

Keep it Simple

Chapter 2.4 Negotiate

Use words everyone can understand. You may have the best vocabulary in the world, but you need to use words that don't require a translator.

Keeping it simple also means setting out your terms clearly. The only way to get to an agreement is to make sure both parties understand the terms.

If you don't understand what your adversary wants, ask for clarification. Just because you don't understand something doesn't make you look stupid. Asking for clarification can actually make you look smart.

Use your adversary's words and phrases when you are speaking or making your presentation. Using their language increases their comfort level. If they think that you understand them and you do, you have a better chance of working out a deal. Always speak to people in their own language when possible.

And then there are times when you should keep your mouth shut. It's OK to be quiet.

Communicating clearly also means weeding out the "fillers" in your speech. Fillers like "ah," "ummm," and

Chapter 2.4 Negotiate

"hmm" can be a distraction. It's hard to remove those extra fillers, but it's incredibly powerful when you do.

It also important to be a good listener, pose a few good questions and listen carefully to the answers. Again, it's smart to prepare those questions in advance.

Make Eye Contact.

If you want to act like a professional, you look people in the eye. Let them know that you are speaking only to them. It is one of the most powerful negotiating tools you can use.

Dress for Success.

Remember what your parents said when you went out to an important occasion? "Make sure your shoes are shined and your suit is pressed."

You should think about fashion, not in a dressy kind of way, but more to think about what your adversary will probably wear. Is this is a casual meeting? Wear something similar. If he's into golf shirts and khaki pants, it would be wise to show up in similar clothing.

Your bearing is also important. Sit up straight and carry yourself with good posture.

Chapter 2.4 Negotiate

Look prepared. If for some reason you don't have any papers to take to the meeting with you, take a pad and pencil so you will look like you are ready for business. And always be on time or a little early for every meeting you go to.

There are also a number of bad habits to avoid.
- Don't fiddle. You might play with your pen or jiggle the coins in your pocket without thinking about it, but it is a huge distraction.
- Don't cut people off mid-sentence. You may think that what you have to say is more important than what the other side has to say. That's wrong. Slow down and let people speak.

Now it's time to negotiate

Responding to an Offer
Here comes your adversary's first offer. There are three ways to respond:
1 Refuse it

Chapter 2.4 Negotiate

2 Take it

3 Present a counteroffer

It can pay to have your adversary make the first offer. Once they have made an offer they feel is fair, you know where they stand and you can go from there. You save time and money you could have lost if you had made the first move.

For example: A strong example.

. A very important point: Write everything down, especially items that you have agreed upon. This is the only way you can keep track of all the aspects of a detailed agreement. Some of the points you negotiate may seem minor, but you want to make sure that they don't come back to be renegotiated.

Also, if you write down each point and your adversary changes his mind and wants to re-open an issue, you can show him that the issue has been agreed upon and resolved. Once something is agreed on and taken off the table, don't let it come back.

When you make an offer or a counteroffer, make sure you are clear about your reasoning so your

Chapter 2.4 Negotiate

adversary understands your position. Clear explanations will strengthen your chances for making a deal.

Example: Write specific example. This way the seller knows you are not just trying to beat him on the price for no reason.

If your first offer is refused, be nice. You just didn't come to an agreement. Keep trying.

Settling at the Best Time

You need to be able to know when it's the best time to reach an agreement. It's crucial to your success.

You have to pay close attention to all the parties involved to pinpoint the right time. When you get there, you extend your hand and it's a deal.

Part of this is practice. The more often you take part in negotiations, the easier it will be for you to recognize the signs of a deal that is about to happen

Here are a few signs the deal isn't ready to be done. Note: when this behavior stops, you can proceed to close the deal.

Chapter 2.4 Negotiate

When your adversary moves away from you in his seat or gets up, he is not ready to continue.

If she holds her head in her hands, or touches her chin, she's not ready.

When your adversary's arms are folded against his chest, it means your message isn't getting through.

When an adversary turns her body away from you, but still looks at you, she's not quite ready to close.

What do you do? Keep talking about your points or ask for more information about their offer. Remind them of the merits and benefits of your offer until you no longer see these signs.

You've agree on a deal. Now you need to put it in writing. The you need to read the entire document several times before signing it. You must know exactly what you are signing. You must understand every word and what each specific phrase means. Now is the time to speak up if you have questions or doubts.

Your best option is to have the contract written according to your specifications and the best way to make sure that happens is to write the contract yourself. The person who writes the deal has a better chance of

Chapter 2.4 Negotiate

getting everything they want in it. Finally, make sure each of the involved parties signs the contract and gets a signed copy.

A little self talk, confidence and attitude.

Building your confidence is a key to a successful negotiation. You started the confidence-building by doing your homework. Because you know the details of the negotiations inside and out, you have the confidence you need get to a successful agreement.

You confidence will also get a boost if you know exactly what you want from the negotiation. Write your objectives down and keep them handy to remind yourself.

You also should build your confidence through self-talk. Write on an index card, "I am a fabulous dealmaker." Do it as far in advance of the negotiation date as you can. Read it often; let it soak into your mind.

Keep reminding yourself of your enthusiasm. Remind yourself that you have the energy to strive for

Chapter 2.4 Negotiate

the best deal that you can and you have the power to reach that goal.

And remind yourself that you can walk away from the negotiating table at any time. Walking away is a powerful tool and it boosts your self-confidence, often to the point where your advers

Being a Power Professional Leader

Chapter 3.1 The Power is in the Plan

"Plans are useless, the planning process is priceless."
..Linda Reed Friedman

Chapter 3.1 The Power is in the Plan

The Power is in The Plan

Chapter 3.1 The Power is in the Plan

I had no grand and glorious goals when I started. I just didn't want to think, behave, or be like that kid from Secaucus that I was. So I had to learn how to dream, to think bigger.

The Dream

The most delightful part of planning is to dream about the goal - achieved in brilliant living color with all the details in place. In your dream, nothing is written. It has a whole range of possibilities. As the dream begins to emerge, it grows as you add another thought, another idea, or another strategy.

The more specific you are as you imagine the outcome of your dream, the more energized and inspired you will become with the possibilities.

The dream is the essence of your life. It is a powerful force and cannot be ignored. Your spirit is the driver. Be motivated by your spirit. Let your imagination run wild. Think of the possibilities. Become enveloped by your vivid, detailed visions.

The dream is your life's work.

Chapter 3.1 The Power is in the Plan

The Importance of Planning

A dream without action is just a dream. The difference between a dream and a goal is that you write the goal down and add specific action steps to achieve it.

> "If you don't know where you are going, any road will get you there."
> ………Lewis Carroll

Write what success looks like to you in one sentence. What is the outcome that you are looking for? Take your time – one sentence is a lot harder than a rambling sheet of ideas. Use words that help you visualize your success.

Once you have decided on your desired outcome, create a list of three objectives that you will need to accomplish to achieve your goal.

Then list three strategies that you will have to put in place to meet your objectives. And last, come up with three tactics for each strategy.

It may be very easy to come up with three objectives. Now you need to question those objectives.

Chapter 3.1 The Power is in the Plan

Ask yourself whether these objectives will really help you reach your goal. Will you reach your goal if you focus on these three objectives or will you be sidetracked by one of them? Will you journey to the goal be faster or slower using these objectives?

Next you need to come up with three strategies for each objective. Again, be very specific. If you need to, do some research to make sure that these strategies are the best for reaching your objectives.

Get rid of your personal feelings. I know it's hard to do because your intuition jumps in, and often it gives you good information. But clear the debris out of your mental plan; start by dealing only with the facts.

One more time with the list of three. Using the strategies, create three tactics; one for each strategy. If you're specific with each step in this process, you will end up with an clear to-do list.

At this point, it pays to remember Murphy's Law: If it can go wrong, it will.

Be productively critical of your plan. Review it carefully the plan and ask yourself, "What can go wrong? Where are the holes? What happens if I miss an

Chapter 3.1 The Power is in the Plan

objective?" You absolutely must know what can possibly keep you from achieving your dream.

As you actively review any potential missteps, figure out what you can do to continue toward your goal if something doesn't go as you planned.

Now estimate how long it might take you to accomplish each of these steps. The length of time can vary greatly, depending on circumstances, so you need to have an idea of when each step can be done compared to when you want it done.

Now that you have everything written down, you should be able to fully understand what it's going to take to reach your goal.

An example of goal writing

Here's your goal: growing a successful garden. To grow a garden, you might come up with the following objectives: soil preparation, buying seedlings, container growing/location

As you think about the summer and reaping the rewards of your garden, you have a dream of a summer

Chapter 3.1 The Power is in the Plan

garden filled with organic Big Boy Rutgers tomatoes. You can taste them.

You remember them from your childhood and you can almost feel them melt in your mouth. The slightly acidic sweetness, the gentle but firm texture of the flesh, the juice that runs down your chin. The thought of having a tomato sandwich on white bread with lettuce and a healthy helping of mayo, makes your mouth water.

So now you have an even more specific garden goal – to grow at least 25 Big Boy tomatoes by the end of August. Here are the objectives that you need to accomplish – prepare the soil, obtain tomato plants or seeds, and figure out where you will plant.

How will you reach these objectives? Next, you need to develop and research your strategies. For example, you want to look into the type of soil mixture is best suited for tomatoes, when to plant tomatoes, where to plant them (directly in the ground or in a container?) Is it better to start with seedlings or with young tomato plants? What weather conditions/location are the best for the best tomatoes?

After you have done the research, you can create a strategy for growing those tomatoes.

Chapter 3.1 The Power is in the Plan

The Strategy

1. Grow a container garden using the soil recommended by
    Rutgers University, New Jersey.
2. Start from seed or purchase seedlings from a grower.
3. Place the container in the right location for optimal growth.

Action steps for:

1. **Grow in a container**......

   Step #1 Soil Prep

   1. Choose right container size with appropriate depth.
   2. Confirm drainage in the bottom of container.
   3. Obtain perfectly balanced growing soil for the Big Boy tomatoes.

   Step # 2 Planting

   1. Grow from seeds or locate a local grower with this specific type of tomato plant.

Chapter 3.1 The Power is in the Plan

2. Use root hormone to encourage growth. Place stakes to support the plants as they grow.
3. Plant at the right time based on your research.

Step #3 Container location

1. Locate container in an area of your yard that gets lots of sun – usually that's southeast.
2. Determine wind patterns and shelter plants if necessary to decrease potential damage.
3. Plan to protect the plants in extreme weather conditions.

Think of alternate action steps: cold frames or greenhouses for seedlings, putting your container on wheels to follow the sun, getting plant lights to augment sunshine.

And if the worst happens and nothing works out the way you planned, you can always find a farm stand and *buy* the tomatoes. ☺

Chapter 3.1 The Power is in the Plan

At each point in your plan, you should ask "What If?" What will happen if I do this? What will happen if I miss a step, or go in another direction? Try to predict the possible outcomes. Explore options for achieving your dream after you have factored in the "what ifs." Your first plan may not be the best and only way of growing Big Boy tomatoes.

Chapter 3.2 Creativity The Foundation of Your Growth

Creativity
The
Foundation of your Growth

Chapter 3.2 Creativity The Foundation of Your Growth

> We don't see things as they are, we see them as *we* are.
> ....Anais Nin

Chapter 3.2 Creativity The Foundation of Your Growth

Creativity

One often overlooked aspect in the development of a power professional is creative thinking. A successful career requires creative thinking. So does starting a business that requires more creativity.

Staying in business requires even more creativity. You need to be creative to stay ahead of prevailing trends if you're not going to be left behind.

For an idea to be creative, it is not enough for it to be innovative. It must also have a positive effect on your business. But how do you generate creative ideas that can grow your business? A few suggestions follow:

Creativity

Creativity is important as a leader. Why? **Creativity answers questions and solves problems.**

1. It is important for a leader to be able to solve problems as the company/organization grows and changes.

Chapter 3.2 Creativity The Foundation of Your Growth

2. A leader needs to be able to communicate to a variety of people. As the world becomes more integrated, cultures merge, and as the diversity of leaders and associates increase.
3. A leaders need to understand what it means to think creatively. He/she needs to understand the process, the timing and the results.
4. A leader needs to recognize creativity within their organization. They need to provide the tools which encourage people to be creative. People are the creative fuel within an organization, it's their ideas that can drive the growth engine.
5. Creativity is also fun.
6. When everyone encouraged is creative using the tools of the artist, the designer and the engineer.

The story about the barber below – a creative essay on creativity. It is a metaphor – like the barber shaving his client – it takes more than one step. More than one "Bright Idea".

Chapter 3.2 Creativity The Foundation of Your Growth

How to Get a Barber Shave at Home ... *Mike Sheehan*

The days of "shave and a haircut – two bits" are long gone. Even I don't remember them, but I do recall getting a barber shave for a sawbuck. Nowadays, a barber shave can set you back 10 times that or more – a bit much to pay for something that's only going to last about a day. If you've ever had a barber shave, though, you know there's nothing that feels as close.

Achieving the same result at home is really impossible, but it's a lot cheaper and you can get something close to a barber shave if you try. Here's how:

The Preparation

If you use a regular razor, put a new blade in it. If you use disposable razors, break out a fresh one.

Take a hot shower.

The Shave

Rinse your face with hot water.

Apply shaving cream, rubbing it into your beard vigorously. Rinse it off with hot water.

Apply shaving cream again and rub it in vigorously.

Wet your razor with hot water.

Start shaving, using short strokes, not long sweeping strokes.

Chapter 3.2 Creativity The Foundation of Your Growth

Rinse the blade frequently to clear it of beard hairs. If you're using a multi-blade razor, tap it against the sink to clear the blades.

After shaving with the grain of your beard, shave against the grain.

Don't be afraid to put some pressure on the razor – don't let it just glide over your beard.

Use sound and touch to make sure you're shaving as closely as you can. You can hear the difference between a blade that is actually cutting through your beard and one that's going over bare skin. Likewise, you can feel the places that you've missed and go over them again.

Rinse off any leftover shaving cream. During the rinse, feel your face again for any spots you may have missed and go over them once more.

Dry your face.

You're done"

Use the Barber Shave as a metaphor to solve problems. How does each step apply to your problem or to your process?

Chapter 3.2 Creativity The Foundation of Your Growth

Elmer R. Gates, (1859-1923) a philosopher, psychologist, scientist, inventor was hired by the brilliant leaders of his day to solve their problems. His key to solving problems was to gather as much information as possible about the company, how it functioned, the people involved and write a very clear statement about the problem. If you can write a very clear statement about the problem, it is almost solved. In Elmer's case, he had a studio. In his studio was a simple wood table, a chair, a lamp he could turn on and off, a set of pencils and a pad.

He would then sit for ideas. When he thought of a possible solution, he would turn on the light and quickly write it down, then turn the lamp off again. He sat in the dark for his ideas, not to be distracted. Leaders need to clarify the problems that are facing them before they can be solved.

It is helpful to use a few creative tools to define and clarify the problems. The more time spent clarifying the circumstances and outlining the problem, the faster it may be solved.

Leadership requires communication with a variety of people. As our world is changing, communication with

Chapter 3.2 Creativity The Foundation of Your Growth

a diverse workforce requires creativity. It especially true that since communication happens in a variety of ways, verbally, visually, written, kinesthetically.

There is more than one way to communicate. It is therefore necessary to explore the possibilities to get the corporate message across to the staff and the branding message across to the potential clients, and to reinforce that message to the existing clients.

A leader needs to understand the creative process in order to get the best, the brightest and the boldest to perform at their highest level. The creative process requires information and lots of it. Information is like soil. It is the growing medium through which the seeds when planted can germinate.

In the case of a tomato seed, we can project almost to the minute exactly when a tomato will be ready to be picked and eaten.

The creative process is not nearly as predictable either in timing or in results. You can gather as much info as possible but yet not be able to determine when a project will be done or if the results will be as you expect. Sometimes a project with all the creativity available is done. The schedule determines the ending.

Chapter 3.2 Creativity The Foundation of Your Growth

A leader needs to be observant of the creative process, understand what is happening in his organization and foster it. Although everyone can be creative, some people generate ideas faster than others from the same information. Speed doesn't necessarily mean better, it just means faster.

A leader can foster ideas by suggesting tools to use and by creating an environment that supports creativity. A humor room, a place to lighten up, a place to rest, a place to gather the stray thoughts into one place, and a place to meditate. This environment is a separate room, one outside the cubicle farms we normally see. When a leader fosters creativity in a person, there is permission for that person to be a little wacky. They may have permission to create a visually stimulating environment and a musically stimulating one. The person or creative team may need access to information available outside the office environment. Or special internet access to high level research programs.

Adding a bit of fun in to the workplace besides, a humor corner; shooting hoops on a Friday afternoon, or an ice cream social in the middle of a hot summer day. Great creativity with fabulous results requires team work.

Chapter 3.2 Creativity The Foundation of Your Growth

As the relationships improve and the staff gets better and better at sharing and communicating with each other the creative results will improve as well.

Everyone was born creative, their creativity has been educated out of them, Sir Ken Robinson **made the point during his Ted TALK "We are educating people out of their creativity,"** He argues that it's because we've been *educated* to become good workers, rather than creative thinkers.

In conclusion – practice, practice, practice. Practice your creativity as much as you can, in the car with the kids, at the piano, in your office at the computer. Stretch yourself.

Verbal Communication

Chapter 3.3 Verbal Communication

"Leaders must be close enough to relate to others, but far enough ahead to motivate them."

...*John C. Maxwell*

Chapter 3.3 Verbal Communication

Being an effective leader requires many skills, not the least of which is the ability to communicate your ideas verbally. Even when you are just talking casually with friends and colleagues, you are delivering a message. Developing good verbal habits can help you improve your image and advance your career.

You may also be asked to speak in more formal occasions. You may be asked to introduce someone to an audience, say thank you for an honor received, give words of encouragement to a beleaguered group of volunteers, or be interviewed as a representative of your company. As you grow in your job, a variety of opportunities will come up and you will be asked to speak. Be prepared to take that opportunity!

Speaking effectively in public doesn't come naturally. It requires dedicated practice and experience.

Here are five simple rules:
- Speak slowly
- Write your speech (do not memorize it)

Chapter 3.3 Verbal Communication

- Rehearse your speech
- Be aware of stage etiquette
- Dress for the occasion

Speak slowly.

There is nothing worse than trying to listen to and understand someone who speaks too quickly. A relaxed pace will make your words heard and understood more easily. A slower pace also helps you get rid of tension and nervousness.

Write your speech.

But before you start writing the speech, first decide what messages you want your audience to remember.
Write those messages first. When I write a speech, I write stories that support the messages I want to convey. Your audience may not remember your message but they will remember your stories.

Chapter 3.3 Verbal Communication

Be Prepared – Rehearse

After I write a speech, I read it out loud to myself. Then I say it out loud, looking at my notes as little as necessary. Then I edit the speech.

I go through this process several times. By the third time, I can usually give the speech without looking at my notes.

As you rehearse, you should also add gestures and choose a spot or spots on the floor where you will deliver the speech.

Now practice your speech three more times with the gestures and floor spots. By now, you've put in a lot of work, but soon you'll find that the speech begins to take on a life of its own.

During a choir rehearsal, Amanda Silliker, a voice coach and choir director, advised her singers, "Now that we know all the notes in the piece, we can make music." That is exactly what happens when you are rehearsing your speech. As you repeat the speech, some parts will get louder and others softer. You start adding gestures;

Chapter 3.3 Verbal Communication

you move around the floor for emphasis. Your speech really does take on a life of its own.

Learn Proper Stage Behavior

When you are invited to be a speaker, there are protocols you will need to follow. For example, you will need to know when it will be your turn so you can be ready to get to the stage when you are introduced. Don't sit in your chair and act surprised as if you had just won an Oscar. You should also bring some energy with you to the stage by moving swiftly. That generates a positive expectation from the audience.

When you reach the stage, wait to be acknowledged by the host, shake their hand and say thank you. At this point, you may realize that you are not ready to begin for a variety of reasons. Ask for help. If you need the lights dimmed, for example. Ask someone to dim them. Don't leave the stage to do it yourself. When you leave the stage, the program feels hollow and empty – stay put and wait.

Chapter 3.3 Verbal Communication

If something happens while you are on stage – a loud noise perhaps, or a waitress drops some dishes, or the lights flicker, acknowledge the incident. Your audience will notice it, so you have to say something about it. If you don't, they'll wonder if you noticed and whether you care about what's happening.

Dress for the speaking occasion

You should dress appropriately for the kind of presentation you are making. Your appearance should be consistent with the subject you're speaking about. You want your speech to be the focus of attention so you should avoid any distracting elements in what you wear.

Wear comfortable shoes and clothes. If you are uncomfortable in what you are wearing, you'll fidget and the audience will see it.

Once your presentation is completed, remain at on stage until your host rejoins you. Then you can leave, unless you are responsible for closing the meeting. If you are, you can leave the stage once you have closed the meeting.

Chapter 3.3 Verbal Communication

A Case Study

What can speaking do for you?

Here's what it did for Neil Biege.

Neil Biege is the former vice president of sales for E.L. Schmidt, Co., a concrete manufacturer. Neil claims that the ability to speak gave him recognition, power, and the position of vice president in his company.

Neil was the person assigned to answer questions when someone asked about his company. Inquiries often came from the organizers of conventions for cement industry officials who were looking for a speaker. Neil would give them a topic he thought would be of interest to the members and volunteer to be the speaker.

The return he received for his public speaking was enormous. The more he spoke, the more people thought of him as an expert in the field. The more conventions he spoke at, the more the visibility of his company increased, and the more sales opportunities came his way. As he acquired more contacts, he learned more about cutting-edge thinking in the industry. He

Chapter 3.3 Verbal Communication

became a thought leader in his field and a thought leader in his company.

Neil's experience should be enough to make you want to add public speaking to your skill set.

More about speaking in public

From my experience as a speaker, I believe you can think at the same time you speak. You can learn how to give yourself time to think when someone asks a question or when you are being interviewed for a job.

When we learned to speak as children, we got into the the habit of filling the empty spaces with "ums" and "ahs." When we get rid of those vocal tics, the empty air space that replaces your "ahs" and "ums" can be used effectively. By taking a deep breath and then speaking, we sound smarter.

And we are smarter because we are using those pauses to think about the best answers and the best way to communicate our ideas.

A leader must learn the rules of speaking in public and learn how to do it well. Public speaking can help you

Chapter 3.3 Verbal Communication

gain greater recognition in your work, whether you work in a corporation or you are a business owner. The more you speak in public, the more powerful and effective your personal presence becomes and that can lead to greater recognition of your talents.

My Experience in Effective Public Speaking

My mom had my sister and I on stage starting at the age of five and up until we were 17. From tap dancing on roller skates to singing a duet, we were always performing in front of people. Because of that background and my experience as a school teacher, a business owner, and as president of various organizations, I could speak in front of a group and not panic. Making a speech was easy, I thought.

Then I joined Toastmasters. Why? We had just moved, I was lonesome and they invited me. Actually Toastmasters had been suggested to me years ago but I blew it off. Bad decision. . When I wrote my first five-minute speech, I thought it would be a snap. To my

Chapter 3.3 Verbal Communication

surprise it wasn't. Instead it was a grueling eight hours of writing and rewriting. My first mistake was to try to fit fifty years into five minutes. The other mistakes are too numerous to mention.

That lesson was truly eye-opening. When I gave that speech, it was bad and I was bad. Just because I didn't faint, have sweaty palms, or run screaming off the stage didn't mean I was informative or funny. On the plus side, because of my childhood stage experience, I was comfortable in front of people.

With good coaching from my fellow toastmasters and lots of support. I eventually wrote a decent speech, kept it with in the five-to-seven-minute time limit, and won a few speech contests.

But when I had to do it again at a higher level within the Toastmasters organization, the wheels came off the bus. I was standing in front of about twenty people at the most. I was giving the speech that I had "given to myself" at least 30 times, I had it memorized it almost word for word (another mistake). I had given it to my local Toastmasters Club and won the club's contest, and I had given it at an Area contest and won.

Chapter 3.3 Verbal Communication

But somehow giving it at the Division level was different. This time it was like an an out-of-body experience. I heard myself speaking and at the same time my mind was screaming. "What the *!#&%!* are you talking about? This isn't not your speech, get back on track, do what we rehearsed!" I didn't and I didn't win that contest.

With lots of practice and a year later, I won 2nd place at the District Level, which is a huge accomplishment in Toastmasters.

So with that background behind me, here are some suggestions that I'd like you to take seriously:

Go to Toastmasters

Write speeches

And practice, practice, practice.

Ultimately, it's not about the contests, it's about getting your message heard. Your messages can be different depending on your audience; they may be for work, your family, or an organization.

Whatever the message, you can't get it heard unless you have one and you have practiced it over and over – and out loud

Conclusion

In Conclusion

If you have followed some of the ideas you learned from this book, you're on your way to creating an image for yourself as a person with a positive internal style. You are a person who is generous with your time and concern as well with your money. You are approachable **and real.**

You are now on your way. You have the tools you need to be a **POWERFUL PROFESSIONAL.**

Why take the journey? Before you begin to make any changes, you should check in with that place deep inside that you defines you. Ask yourself to consider why it is important for you to change.

Some of the suggestions in this book are simple but they aren't easy. A few of these suggestions may take a long time to achieve results, but the effort can be worth it.

Think about the benefits of change to make sure you are willing to begin a journey of change for yourself. A long look at where you want to be, a look at the

Conclusion

dreams you had as a child is a good beginning. That's the past. Now, write your life as you see it in the future.

You can make it happen but not without a road map. Without a map, you can end up anywhere – from a Bowery flophouse to a penthouse on Park Avenue. But with a plan, you can choose your destination.

Be Creative

A creative approach helps you to be a power professional. Keep your mind open to all the possibilities. Use creative tools to solve problems and answer questions. Use them all the time, from the smallest problem to the largest question. Creative thinking keeps you mentally alert and open-minded to solutions that you hadn't considered.

Manage Your Time

"What's the best use of my time?" is a question we ask ourselves often. How can I use the time I have available to me today grow my company or my career?

Conclusion

We tend look at one day at a time without paying attention to the bigger picture. What happens then is that our time gets used up by other people. They squander our time with meaningless appointments, unscheduled meetings, and meetings that go too long or have no agenda.

Take the time to plan your year. ATT plans their facilities for five years and they are thrilled if they get six months use out of them. Plan your own life and business for two years, and be happy for six months of progress.

Then look at your time again, using a shorter time frame. What do you hope to accomplish this week that will move everything towards your goal? If you plan the use of your time with a purpose, you are in control.

During the course of my career, I was attending a lot of meetings that dragged on. I became more impatient with the time I was wasting, so I created a few boundaries for myself and my committees.

My first rule was to leave after one hour, no matter what kind of progress the committee had made. If the leaders hadn't come up with an agenda for the meeting, the chances of getting anything done were

Conclusion

slim. But lack of planning on their part was no reason for me to waste my time.

Build a Great Team

It is a team of people who help all the big dreamers of the world reach their goals. We all need a team to help us move our dream forward. Our best plans may not see the light of day without a willing team to help us.

Because of that, attention to our team is one of the most important jobs we have. We are the guardians of their talent and are responsible for a building a creative, productive environment for them. They are the artisans behind the scenes making what you do appear effortless. Take care of them.

Some simple team leadership tips:

Ask for help. Give everybody a job to do. Be nurturing. Be a cheerleader. Keep your cool. Have fun for no reason. And every once in a while, be outrageous and surprise them with humor.

And There's More . . .

Conclusion

Let's review some of the other suggestions in this book.

Negotiating

When you are going into a negotiation, prepare yourself. Research the situation and the people involved, level the playing field by asking a few "what if's," and when it's time to negotiate, give yourself a confidence-building self talk. Confidence wins as many battles as knowledge.

Bearing and Communication

Stand up straight, look people in the eye, shake hands with some enthusiasm. Do the exercises in the work book. They will help advance the new you faster.

Convention

Knowing the protocols of daily life can save us from embarrassment. It can also give you a more polished, positive and proficient image.

Image – Branding

Learn who you are. If you like yourself, you're off to a great start. If you don't, take time to learn who you

Conclusion

would like to be. Some of us need to do a lot of work on this; some of us not as much. It is your inside Image that you need to work on first. It's is easier to create of positive outer image and behave accordingly once you know who you are and who you want to be.

Verbal Communication

Learning to speak and hold an audience's attention is another key to your success. Whether you are talking about good news or bad news, or giving a product update or just doing a standup routine, learn the ropes, polish your speeches and have fun.

Being Successful

Striving towards success means using all these tools and using them as often as you possibly can. Then you will become the unsurpassed person you are.

Being a powerful professional means being genuine, resolute in attaining the vision for your life, determined, and thoughtful. But is also means being ready to laugh, have fun, and enjoy the journey.

References

The tools you need to create a successful business are between the pages. Read for about fifteen minutes every day. Good Luck!

- ◆ Growing your Business – Mark LeBlanc
- ◆ The Greatest Salesman in the World – Og Mandino
- ◆ Thinking on your Feet – Marian k. Woodall
- ◆ Gung Ho – Ken Blanchard, Sheldon Bowles
- ◆ Million Dollar Consulting – Alan Weiss (anything by Alan)
- ◆ Think and Grow Rich – Napoleon Hill
- ◆ How I raised myself from failure to success in selling – Frank Bettinger
- ◆ The 22 Biggest Mistakes Mangers Make and how to correct them – James K. Van Fleet
- ◆ Book Yourself Solid – Michael Port
- ◆ The War of Art – Steven Pressfield
- ◆ A Wack on the Side of the Head – Roger von Oech
- ◆ Negotiating for Dummies – Donaldson

References

- The Facilitators Field Book – Justice and Jamieson
- Blue Ocean Strategy – W. Chan Kim and Renee Maugorgne
- The One minute Mangers Build High Performing Teams,- Blanchard, Carew, Parisi-Carew
- The 9 steps to Financial Freedom – Suze Orman
- 1001 Way to Energize Employees – Bob Nelson
- Tony Robbins – his life's work.
- Made to Stick – Chip Health and Dan Health
- Creating Magic – Lee Cockerell
- Lean In - Sheryl Sandberg
- Zig Ziglar on Selling - Zig Ziglar (anything by Zig)
- Book Yourself Solid – Michael Port
- Get Clients Now – C. J. Hayden
- Brian Tracy